Whistleblowers

Other Books of Related Interest:

Opposing Viewpoints Series:

The Banking Crisis
Corporate Social Responsibility
Ethics
White Collar Crime

At Issue Series:

Corporate Corruption

Current Controversies Series:

Espionage and Intelligence
Jobs in America

> "Congress shall make no law … abridging the freedom of speech, or of the press."

First Amendment to the US Constitution

The basic foundation of our democracy is the First Amendment guarantee of freedom of expression. The Opposing Viewpoints Series is dedicated to the concept of this basic freedom and the idea that it is more important to practice it than to enshrine it.

OPPOSING
VIEWPOINTS®
SERIES

Whistleblowers

Noah Berlatsky, Book Editor

GREENHAVEN PRESS
A part of Gale, Cengage Learning

GALE
CENGAGE Learning·

Detroit • New York • San Francisco • New Haven, Conn • Waterville, Maine • London

Elizabeth Des Chenes, *Director, Publishing Solutions*

© 2012 Greenhaven Press, a part of Gale, Cengage Learning

Articles in Greenhaven Press anthologies are often edited for length to meet page requirements. In addition, original titles of these works are changed to clearly present the main thesis and to explicitly indicate the author's opinion. Every effort is made to ensure that Greenhaven Press accurately reflects the original intent of the authors. Every effort has been made to trace the owners of copyrighted material.

Cover image © Monalyn Gracia/Fancy/Corbis.

LIBRARY OF CONGRESS CATALOGING-IN-PUBLICATION DATA

Whistleblowers / Noah Berlatsky, book editor.
     p. cm. -- (Opposing viewpoints)
     Includes bibliographical references and index.
     ISBN 978-0-7377-6346-1 (hardcover) -- ISBN 978-0-7377-6347-8 (pbk.)
  1. Whistle blowing. I. Berlatsky, Noah.
     HD60.W485 2012
     342.73'068--dc23

2012004995

Printed in the United States of America
1 2 3 4 5 6 7 16 15 14 13 12

Contents

Why Consider Opposing Viewpoints?   **11**

Introduction   **14**

Chapter 1: What Motivates Whistleblowers?

Chapter Preface   **18**

1. Whistle-Blowers' Experiences in Fraud Litigation
   Against Pharmaceutical Companies   **20**
   *Aaron S. Kesselheim, David M. Studdert, and
   Michelle M. Mello*

2. Whistleblowers May Have Moral and
   Immoral Motivations   **40**
   Matthias Kleinhempel

3. Whistleblowers May Be Motivated by Revenge
   to Make False Accusations   **46**
   Mark Bisson

4. Rewards Give Whistleblowers a Motivation to
   Reveal Wrongdoing   **50**
   Stephen Martin Kohn

5. Reward Programs Do Not Motivate Whistleblowers   **62**
   Jonathan L. Awner and Denise Dickins

Periodical and Internet Sources Bibliography   **72**

Chapter 2: Do Whistleblowers Compromise National Security?

Chapter Preface   **74**

1. Those Who Expose National Secrets Should
   Be Punished   **76**
   Gabriel Schoenfeld

2. Whistleblowers Expose Illegal Activity, Not
   Government Secrets   87
   Jesselyn Radack

3. Whistleblower Thomas Drake Compromised
   Classified Information   97
   United States Department of Justice

4. The Prosecution of Whistleblower Thomas Drake
   Is Unjust   102
   Jane Mayer

5. Whistleblowers Can Endanger National
   Food Supplies   114
   *Annette Sweeney, interviewed by Katerina
   Lorenzatos Makris*

6. Whistleblowers Help Protect National Food Supplies   119
   Sarah Damian

Periodical and Internet Sources Bibliography   124

Chapter 3: Does WikiLeaks Perform a Valuable Function as a Whistleblower?

Chapter Preface   126

1. WikiLeaks's Government Document Leaks Are
   Vital for Democracy   128
   Daniel Ellsberg, interviewed by Brad Friedman

2. WikiLeaks's Government Document Leaks Are a
   Danger to Democracy   137
   CIGI

3. Alleged WikiLeaks Whistleblower Bradley Manning
   Is a Hero   143
   Chase Madar

4. WikiLeaks Whistleblowers Are Traitors   152
   Michael Reagan

Periodical and Internet Sources Bibliography   156

Chapter 4: What Consequences Do Whistleblowers Face?

Chapter Preface   158

1. Organizations Often Defend Themselves by
   Attacking Whistleblowers   160
   David Hutton

2. Organizations Do Not Help Themselves by
   Attacking Whistleblowers   168
   Suzanne Lucas

3. For One Whistle-Blower, No Good Deed
   Goes Unpunished   172
   Jesse Eisinger

4. An Expert in Government Contracting Faces
   Reprisals for Whistleblowing   177
   Bunnatine H. Greenhouse

Periodical and Internet Sources Bibliography   182

For Further Discussion   183

Organizations to Contact   185

Bibliography of Books   190

Index   194

Why Consider Opposing Viewpoints?

> *"The only way in which a human being can make some approach to knowing the whole of a subject is by hearing what can be said about it by persons of every variety of opinion and studying all modes in which it can be looked at by every character of mind. No wise man ever acquired his wisdom in any mode but this."*
>
> John Stuart Mill

In our media-intensive culture it is not difficult to find differing opinions. Thousands of newspapers and magazines and dozens of radio and television talk shows resound with differing points of view. The difficulty lies in deciding which opinion to agree with and which "experts" seem the most credible. The more inundated we become with differing opinions and claims, the more essential it is to hone critical reading and thinking skills to evaluate these ideas. Opposing Viewpoints books address this problem directly by presenting stimulating debates that can be used to enhance and teach these skills. The varied opinions contained in each book examine many different aspects of a single issue. While examining these conveniently edited opposing views, readers can develop critical thinking skills such as the ability to compare and contrast authors' credibility, facts, argumentation styles, use of persuasive techniques, and other stylistic tools. In short, the Opposing Viewpoints Series is an ideal way to attain the higher-level thinking and reading skills so essential in a culture of diverse and contradictory opinions.

In addition to providing a tool for critical thinking, Opposing Viewpoints books challenge readers to question their own strongly held opinions and assumptions. Most people form their opinions on the basis of upbringing, peer pressure, and personal, cultural, or professional bias. By reading carefully balanced opposing views, readers must directly confront new ideas as well as the opinions of those with whom they disagree. This is not to argue simplistically that everyone who reads opposing views will—or should—change his or her opinion. Instead, the series enhances readers' understanding of their own views by encouraging confrontation with opposing ideas. Careful examination of others' views can lead to the readers' understanding of the logical inconsistencies in their own opinions, perspective on why they hold an opinion, and the consideration of the possibility that their opinion requires further evaluation.

Evaluating Other Opinions

To ensure that this type of examination occurs, Opposing Viewpoints books present all types of opinions. Prominent spokespeople on different sides of each issue as well as well-known professionals from many disciplines challenge the reader. An additional goal of the series is to provide a forum for other, less known, or even unpopular viewpoints. The opinion of an ordinary person who has had to make the decision to cut off life support from a terminally ill relative, for example, may be just as valuable and provide just as much insight as a medical ethicist's professional opinion. The editors have two additional purposes in including these less known views. One, the editors encourage readers to respect others' opinions—even when not enhanced by professional credibility. It is only by reading or listening to and objectively evaluating others' ideas that one can determine whether they are worthy of consideration. Two, the inclusion of such viewpoints encourages the important critical thinking skill of objectively evaluating an author's credentials and bias. This evaluation will illuminate an author's reasons for taking a particular stance on an issue and will aid in readers' evaluation of the author's ideas.

It is our hope that these books will give readers a deeper understanding of the issues debated and an appreciation of the complexity of even seemingly simple issues when good and honest people disagree. This awareness is particularly important in a democratic society such as ours in which people enter into public debate to determine the common good. Those with whom one disagrees should not be regarded as enemies but rather as people whose views deserve careful examination and may shed light on one's own.

Thomas Jefferson once said that "difference of opinion leads to inquiry, and inquiry to truth." Jefferson, a broadly educated man, argued that "if a nation expects to be ignorant and free . . . it expects what never was and never will be." As individuals and as a nation, it is imperative that we consider the opinions of others and examine them with skill and discernment. The Opposing Viewpoints Series is intended to help readers achieve this goal.

David L. Bender and Bruno Leone,
Founders

Introduction

"[Mark] Felt believed he was protecting the bureau by finding a way, clandestine as it was, to push some of the information from the FBI interviews and files out to the public, to help build public and political pressure to make [President Richard] Nixon and his people answerable."

> Bob Woodward, "How Mark Felt Became 'Deep Throat',"
> Washington Post, June 2, 2005.

One of the most famous whistleblowers in history was a man named Deep Throat. That was not his real name; it was a pseudonym taken from a pornographic movie. The man given the name Deep Throat was an informant who provided *Washington Post* reporter Bob Woodward with information about illegal activities conducted by President Richard Nixon and his staff. Among other things, the Nixon White House arranged a break-in at Democratic National Committee headquarters in the Watergate complex and then attempted to cover it up. This became known as the Watergate Scandal. It eventually led to Nixon's resignation.

Bob Woodward described several vivid meetings with Deep Throat in *All the President's Men*, a book written with reporter Carl Bernstein about the investigation of Watergate. Here is one passage:

Deep Throat was waiting. He looked worn, but was smiling. "What's up?" he asked mock-offhandedly, and took a deep drag on his cigarette. Just once, Woodward wished, Deep

Throat would really tell him what was up—everything, no questions asked, no tug of wills, a full status report. . . . Each time Woodward had raised the question, Deep Throat had gravely insisted, "I have to do this my way."

The mysterious portrait of Deep Throat sparked much speculation about his identity. The debate only intensified over the decades—Woodward refused to reveal the name of his source for thirty years. Mark Feldstein, in an August/September 2004 essay in *American Journalism Review*, listed some of the leading suspects. These included Nixon's former chief of staff General Alexander Haig; Nixon's advisor David Gergen; and Nixon's speechwriter and later presidential candidate Patrick Buchanan. Some (though not Feldstein) even speculated that Nixon's assistant attorney general, and later Supreme Court justice, William Rehnquist may have been Deep Throat.

Finally, however, Deep Throat revealed himself. In 2005, Mark Felt, the number two official in the Federal Bureau of Investigation (FBI) during the Nixon administration, admitted that he had been Woodward's source during the Watergate investigation.

Though everyone now knew that Felt was Deep Throat, his motivations for becoming Deep Throat remained unclear. Felt's 2008 obituary in the *New York Times* offered a number of overlapping explanations. First, the obituary said, Felt had leaked information to Woodward because Nixon had put pressure on the FBI to back off of the Watergate investigation. Felt believed that this was "an effort to obstruct justice, and he rejected it," according to the *Times*. The *Times* also suggested that Felt's anger at Nixon may have been caused because Nixon had passed over Felt for the position of director of the FBI. Felt said Nixon wanted to "convert the bureau into an adjunct of the White House machine," as quoted in the *Times*.

The revelation that Deep Throat was Mark Felt prompted much controversy. After Felt's confession, many of Nixon's aides came forward to lambast him for speaking to the press about the

Watergate scandal. Former Nixon speechwriter Pat Buchanan suggested in a June 1, 2005, interview on *MSNBC* that the early termination of Nixon's presidency resulted in the Cambodian genocide and that Felt should feel responsible for those deaths. "I think that Mark Felt was ashamed at what he did," Buchanan said. "That's why he lied about it for 30 years, and he ought to have been." Chuck Colson, a former Nixon advisor, said in the same interview, "I think he goes out on a very sour note, he goes out of his life on a very sour note, not as a hero." Others have pointed out that Felt himself, while working at the FBI, authorized illegal wiretaps of the radical group the Weather Underground, actions for which he was convicted and later pardoned. Felt has also been criticized for his opposition to allowing women into the FBI.

Whatever Felt's personal failings, however, many have argued that he should be praised for leaking information about Watergate. For example, Brendan Miniter in a June 7, 2005, article in the *Wall Street Journal* argued that under Nixon "corruption in government had become rampant" and that Felt did the country an important service by revealing this corruption to the American people. Similarly, the *Philadelphia Enquirer* in a December 23, 2008, article argued that Felt's death was "a reminder of the importance of courageous whistleblowers and a robust media." Certainly, few whistleblowers have had such a direct and lasting impact as Felt, whose revelations toppled the president of the United States.

Opposing Viewpoints: Whistleblowers examines the questions and controversies surrounding whistleblowers in chapters titled What Motivates Whistleblowers? Do Whistleblowers Compromise National Security? Does WikiLeaks Perform a Valuable Function as a Whistleblower? and What Consequences Do Whistleblowers Face? Authors offer different perspectives on whether whistleblowers such as Deep Throat are heroes or villains and whether they protect or harm the public.

OPPOSING VIEWPOINTS® SERIES

CHAPTER 1

What Motivates Whistleblowers?

Chapter Preface

A whistleblower may be motivated by a desire for justice or by a concern for public safety. He or she may also be motivated by a cash reward or a desire for revenge against personal enemies. A less discussed, but sometimes important, motivation can be religion.

Eamon Javers, in a February 12, 2011, CNBC article, reported that religion is often an important inspiration for whistleblowers. Javers said that an important factor is that religious people have an identity outside their job. This can give them a grounding that allows them to recognize and report on wrongdoing. Javers quotes Cheryl Eckard, a whistleblower who reported wrongdoing by pharmaceutical company GlaxoSmithKline, as saying, "it helps to have faith, you know, in something. You have to believe in something. And for me, my faith in God carried me through this. I prayed my way through it."

In a 2002 article in the *Journal of Business Ethics*, Colin Grant also linked religion with whistleblowing. Grant argued that the moral strength required of whistleblowers is so far outside the norms of secular culture that it really makes sense only in a religious context.

Grant admits that some whistleblowers may report abuses for the money or out of motives of revenge, but he concludes that "the most serious instances [of whistleblowing] involve a level of moral sensitivity that approaches religious proportions." He adds that such self-sacrifice in the interest of morality "is baffling for a culture that has dispensed with sainthood."

Some writers have rejected the idea that whistleblowers are especially likely to be religious, however. Margaret Heffernan writing in a February 8, 2011, article on CBS News, for example, reported that academics have not had much success in identifying common traits of whistleblowers. Heffernan says whistleblowers are not necessarily more likely to be women than men, and they are also not "consistently religious, anti-religious, young, old, radical, or crazy." Whereas Javers's article suggests that whistleblowers are those with a loyalty outside the corporation, Hefferman argues that whistleblowers usually "start off as true believers, devoted to the institutions that they serve."

The viewpoints in the following chapter further examine the motivations and morality of whistleblowing.

> "A majority [of whistleblowers]
> perceived their net recovery to be small
> relative to the time they spent on the
> case and the disruption and damage to
> their careers."

Whistle-Blowers' Experiences in Fraud Litigation Against Pharmaceutical Companies

Aaron S. Kesselheim, David M. Studdert, and Michelle M. Mello

Aaron S. Kesselheim is an assistant professor at Harvard Medical School. David M. Studdert is an adjunct associate professor, and Michelle M. Mello is a professor at the Harvard School of Public Health. The following viewpoint focuses on pharmaceutical whistleblowers who aided in federal investigations and received compensation. The authors find that most whistleblowers were motivated by moral factors. The authors say that financial rewards did not repay whistleblowers for the damage to their careers and health. The authors conclude that for moral reasons the whistleblowers still largely felt that they were right to pursue the investigations.

As you read, consider the following questions:

1. How many interviews do the authors say they conducted, and how long was the average length of each interview?

2. What was the most cited motivation for whistleblowers, according to the authors?

3. According to the authors, what was the range of financial rewards received by the whistleblowers and what was the median award?

Prosecution and prevention of health care fraud and abuse are essential to reducing U.S. health care spending.[1-3] A number of recent high-profile cases have uncovered suspect business practices and led to substantial recoveries; in September 2009, for example, Pfizer paid $2.3 billion to settle allegations that it marketed its drugs illegally to physicians, leading to unnecessary payments by the government.[4]

Currently, 90% of health care fraud cases are "qui tam" actions in which whistle-blowers with direct knowledge of the alleged fraud initiate the litigation on behalf of the government.[5] Qui tam derives from the Latin phrase *qui tam pro domino rege quam pro se ipso in hac parte sequitur*, meaning "who as well for the king as for himself sues in this matter." If a qui tam action leads to a financial recovery, the whistle-blower stands to collect a portion of the award. From 1996 through 2005, qui tam

1. Iglehart JK. Finding money for health care reform—rooting out waste, fraud, and abuse. N Engl J Med 2009;361:229–231.

2. Health insurance: vulnerable payers lose billions to fraud and abuse. Washington, DC: General Accounting Office, May 1992. (Publication no. GAO/HRD-92-69.) (Accessed April 22, 2010, at http://archive.gao.gov/t2pbat6/146547.pdf.)

3. Sparrow MK. License to steal: how fraud bleeds America's health care system. Boulder, CO: Westview Press, 2000.

4. Harris G. Pfizer pays $2.3 billion to settle marketing case. New York Times. September 2, 2009:B4.

5. Fraud statistics—overview: October 1, 1986, to September 30, 2007. Washington, DC: Civil Division, Department of Justice, November 2007. (Accessed April 22, 2010, at http://www.taf.org/STATS-FY-2007.pdf.)

actions led to more than $9 billion in recoveries.[6] Although such actions are touted as cost-effective[7] and may deter inappropriate behavior,[8] little is known about how well the qui tam process works.

From their vantage point at the center of the process, whistle-blowers have valuable insights. Popular portrayals of whistle-blowers vary widely: some anecdotes paint them as heroes struggling against corporate greed, emphasizing the hardships and retaliation they must endure; other accounts question their motives and the "excessive" rewards they receive.[9-14]

The goal of this study is to shed light on the motivations and experiences of whistle-blowers in cases of major health care fraud. We conducted interviews with whistle-blowers who were key informants in recent prosecutions brought against pharmaceutical manufacturers. Enforcement actions against pharmaceutical manufacturers have become the most lucrative type of health care fraud litigation on the basis of recovery amounts (average and gross).[6, 15, 16]

6. Kesselheim AS, Studdert DM. Whistleblower-initiated enforcement actions against health care fraud and abuse in the United States, 1996–2005. Ann Intern Med 2008;149:342–349
7. Meyer JA. Fighting Medicare fraud: more bang for the federal buck. Washington, DC: Taxpayers against fraud, July 2006. (Accessed April 22, 2010, at http://www.taf.org/FCA-2006report.pdf.)
8. Becker D, Kessler D, McClellan M. Detecting Medicare abuse. J Health Econ 2005;24:189–210
9. Lenzer J. What can we learn from medical whistleblowers? PLoS Med 2005;2:e209-e209
10. Rost P. The whistleblower: confessions of a health care hitman. Brooklyn, NY: Soft Skull Press, 2006.
11. Alford CF. Whistleblowers: broken lives and organizational power. Ithaca, NY: Cornell University Press, 2002.
12. Glazer MP, Glazer PM. The whistleblowers: exposing corruption in government and industry. New York: Basic Books, 1989.
13. Brenner M. The man who knew too much. Vanity Fair. May 1996:170–92.
14. Glazer M. Ten whistleblowers and how they fared. Hastings Cent Rep 1983;13:33–41
15. Mello MM, Studdert DM, Brennan TA. Shifting terrain in the regulation of off-label promotion of pharmaceuticals. N Engl J Med 2009;360:1557–1566
16. Sandburg B. Health care fraud investigations bedevil Pharma industry: if you're not under investigation, it's only because you've recently settled. The Pink Sheet. November 16, 2009:21–4. (Bridgewater, NJ: Elsevier Business Intelligence.)

Study Methods

Officials in the Civil Division of the U.S. Department of Justice helped us identify 17 federal qui tam cases against pharmaceutical manufacturers settled between January 2001 and March 2009 (Table 1). Using the unsealed complaints and settlement agreements, as well as direct approaches to attorneys involved in the litigation, we identified 42 whistle-blowers involved in these cases. We conducted individual, semistructured interviews with 26 (62%) of them. The interviews had a median duration of 40 minutes (interquartile range, 31 to 49) and addressed the whistle-blowers' motivations and experiences. We analyzed the interview transcripts using the constant comparative method of qualitative analysis.[17, 18] A detailed description of the study methods is provided in the Supplementary Appendix, available with the full text of this article at NEJM.org.

Overview of the Qui Tam Litigation Process

The federal False Claims Act (FCA) prohibits the submission of false claims or statements to the government. Violators face fines of $5,500 to $11,000 per claim, plus treble damages. Whistle-blowers (referred to as relators) can initiate cases by filing a sealed complaint in federal court, nearly always with the help of a personal attorney. In our sample, 22 (85%) were employees of the defendant company (insiders), including 9 at the executive or midmanagerial level and 13 lower-level employees.

The Justice Department then investigates the allegations, often in conjunction with other interested agencies. If the evidence supports the allegations, the Justice Department may elect to intervene and take the lead in the enforcement action. When

17. Bradley EH, Holmboe ES, Mattera JA, Roumanis SA, Radford MJ, Krumholz HM. A qualitative study of increasing beta-blocker use after myocardial infarction: why do some hospitals succeed? JAMA 2001;285:2604–2611
18. Willms DG, Best JA, Taylor DW, et al. A systematic approach for using qualitative methods in primary prevention research. Med Anthropol Q 1990;4:391–409

Table 1. Whistle-Blower–Initiated Federal Pharmaceutical Fraud Cases Settled Between January 2001 and March 2009

Company and Year	Settlement (millions of $)	Drug	Summary of Alleged Improper Conduct
TAP, 2001	875	Lupron	Inflated government reimbursement for prescription of its drug by reporting average wholesale price as significantly higher than the average sales price
Warner-Lambert, 2003	49	Lipitor and others	Violated best-price rules by offering rebates to private insurers*; gave kickbacks to private insurers for favoring drug on formularies
AstraZeneca, 2003	335	Zoladex	Inflated government reimbursement for prescription of its drug by reporting average wholesale price as significantly higher than the average sales price
Bayer, 2003	257	Cipro and Adalat CC	Sold relabeled drugs to private payers at discounted prices and then concealed this information to avoid obligation to pay such rebates to the government
Warner-Lambert, 2004	430	Neurontin	Aggressively marketed drug for off-label indications; gave kickbacks to high-prescribing physicians; made false statements about safety

* Best-price rules state that Medicaid must be granted the lowest price for drugs offered to any private purchaser.

Table 1 (continued)

Company and Year	Settlement (millions of $)	Drug	Summary of Alleged Improper Conduct
Schering-Plough, 2004	346	Claritin	Offered underpriced and free goods and services to private sector that it did not offer to government programs
GlaxoSmithKline, 2005	150	Zofran and Kytril	Inflated government reimbursement for prescription of its drug by reporting average wholesale price as significantly higher than average sales price
Serono, 2005	704	Serostim	Paid kickbacks to induce prescribing and falsified bioelectrical impedance analysis test results to make patients appear to be candidates for drug
King, 2005	124	Altace, Levoxyl, and others	Submitted inaccurate price data to the government, resulting in rebate amounts on its drug products that were lower than they should have been
InterMune, 2006	17	Actimmune	Conducted off-label marketing, including making false statements about drug efficacy to induce prescription writing and creating a "safety registry" to facilitate off-label sales
Bristol-Myers Squibb, 2007	515	Pravachol, Glucophage, and others	Conducted off-label marketing, including using misleading reprints and other sources, inducing prescription writing by offering rebates and gifts to off-label prescribing physicians, and holding continuing medical education meetings to induce writing of unapproved prescriptions

Table 1 (continued)

Company and Year	Drug	Settlement (millions of $)	Summary of Alleged Improper Conduct
Cell Therapeutics, 2007	Trisenox	11	Conducted off-label marketing, including suppression of data about a dangerous side effect (acute promyelocytic leukemia differentiation syndrome) and manipulation of efficacy studies
Orphan Medical, 2007	Xyrem	20	Conducted off-label marketing, including organizing continuing medical education events with speakers describing unapproved uses of the drug and teaching physicians to falsify billing codes
Medicis, 2007	Loprox	10	Conducted off-label marketing of an antifungal cream, approved for use in adults, for the treatment of diaper rash in children; misrepresented safety data
Merck, 2008	Vioxx and Pepcid	650	Failed to pay proper rebates to government programs and paid providers to induce prescriptions through payments for training, consultation, or research
Cephalon, 2008	Provigil, Gabitrill, and Actiq	425	Conducted off-label marketing, including active help in securing government reimbursement for prescriptions for unapproved uses
Eli Lilly, 2009	Zyprexa and others	1,400	Conducted off-label marketing to children and to elderly patients in long-term care facilities; failed to provide information about drugs' side effects

multiple parties file complaints about the same activity, the first to file is assigned the role of the "lead relator," but other relators who provide useful evidence may be included. Almost all cases in which the Justice Department intervenes result in judgments against or settlements with the defendant. For the relators in our sample, cases took an average of 4.9 years (range, 1 to 9) from filing to closure.

Under the FCA, relators are eligible to receive 15 to 25% of the recovery. The total relator share is set by the government and then divided among relators. The recovery may be withheld if the relator was involved in generating the allegedly fraudulent activity. After attorney's fees and taxes, 5 of the relators in our sample received less than $1 million in financial recoveries from their case, 13 received between $1 million and $5 million, and 7 received more than $5 million (1 relator did not provide net estimates).

If the government decides not to intervene, the case may remain sealed and is often dismissed. Whistle-blowers may press forward alone (and earn up to 30% of any recovery), but in practice, solo actions rarely result in substantial recoveries.

Relators' Accounts of the Experience

Discovery of and Initial Reactions to the Alleged Fraud. The relators we interviewed became aware of the troubling corporate behavior in a variety of ways. Whereas all 4 of the "outsiders" came across it in their normal course of business, the triggering event for most (16 of 22) insiders was a career change—starting at a new company (10 of 16) or being promoted to a new position (6 of 16). Changes in the business environment, such as increased competition or new management after a corporate takeover or merger, also contributed to bringing the alleged fraud to relators' attention. One relator described a time when her employer's highest-earning product faced generic competition: "It wasn't until there were extreme competitive pressures and negative effects on earnings that the company's marketing practices became much more aggressive" (Relator 14).

Initially, a large proportion (11 of 26) of the relators refused to participate in the corporate actions that led to the suit. Insiders who took this course reported that their job performances began lagging relative to that of their peers, whose sales were enhanced by the marketing schemes. Nearly all (18 of 22) insiders first tried to fix matters internally by talking to their superiors, filing an internal complaint, or both. One explained: "At first it was to the head of my department, the national sales director, and the national marketing director. . . . After being shooed aside, I went to the executive vice president over all the divisions of sales and marketing. Then eventually I went to the CEO of the company, the chief medical officer, and the president" (Relator 7). Insiders who voiced concerns were met with assertions that the proposed behavior was legal (4 of 22) and dismissals of their complaints, with accompanying demands that the relators do what they were told (12 of 22).

Motivations. Although the relators in this sample all ended up using the qui tam mechanism, only six specifically intended to do so. The others fell into the qui tam process after seeking lawyers for other reasons (e.g., unfair employment practices) or after being encouraged to file suit by family or friends. Every relator we interviewed stated that the financial bounty offered under the federal statute had not motivated their participation in the qui tam lawsuit. Reported motivations coalesced around four non-mutually exclusive themes: integrity, altruism or public safety, justice, and self-preservation (Table 2).

The most common of the themes, integrity (11 of 26 relators), was linked by some relators to their individual personality traits and strong ethical standards. One relator reasoned, "When I lodged my initial complaint with the company, I believed what we were doing was unethical and only technically illegal. This ethical transgression drove my decision. My peers could live with the implications of 'doing 60 in a 55 mph zone' because it did indeed seem trivial. However, my personal betrayal . . . so

Table 2. Primary Motivations for Initiating Qui Tam Lawsuit

Motivation*	Illustrative Remark
Self-preservation (reported by 5 relators)	"If these guys go down I'm not going to be the one that gets blamed for all of this." (Relator 5)
	"Then in the end they were pushing me to break some more laws. I had just said, 'I'm putting my foot down. I'm being excluded from meetings. They're making decisions that I'm going to do things that are illegal'. So I felt like they were just trying to set me up." (Relator 6)
	"I thought, 'I'm involved in something that's illegal. This is dangerous to people.... Maybe I'm—am I going to get arrested?'" (Relator 11)
Justice (reported by 7 relators)	"[I] was proud to be involved in it because we thought we were on the right side of justice here.... this was an illegal activity that needed to be reported." (Relator 2)
	"Shame on them. They should be held accountable for the way they treat people. They should be held accountable for their illegal and unethical behavior." (Relator 12)
	"I think it's our responsibility. It's our duty. It's not an act of heroism. It's not an act of bravery. It's an act of responsibility." (Relator 24)

Table 2 (continued)

Motivation*	Illustrative Remark
Integrity (reported by 11 relators)	"This doesn't just hurt patients and physicians and give industry a bad name. This hurts everybody, whether you're a shareholder [or] a retiree with a pension from them. Everybody's taking a whack on this." (Relator 4)
	"It was just something that I knew was wrong. I needed to correct it." (Relator 15)
	"This is not right. We have laws to protect people from this, to protect the public from this . . . so I needed to stand up for my rights not only for every other person in this company but for my young daughters coming after me starting careers." (Relator 22)
	"I was angry they were trying to get me to do something wrong." (Relator 23)
Altruism or public safety (reported by 7 relators)	"I've got autopsy reports. I've got multiple physician confirmations. I've got the chief medical officer who sent me an email saying, 'Yes. [The side effect] is occurring.' . . . Then they demoted me? I knew there was a problem. That's when I decided to go down that road." (Relator 7)
	"I think if it had been a drug that was like a cream for diaper rash or something like that I don't know that I would've been so idealistic and bold and brave. . . . I don't think I've got that great of character to be honest with you. But I think this drug kind of scared me. I didn't want to be responsible for somebody dying." (Relator 11)
	"This was really asking programs designed for the poorest among us to underwrite a company whose profit rates were pushing 20%. The whole deal was being subsidized by programs for the poor." (Relator 16)

* Some relators identified with more than one source of motivation.

filled me with shame that I could not live with this seemingly trivial violation" (Relator 25). The relators in this group felt that financial circumstances helped to subvert such ethical standards in their colleagues, saying that most colleagues were unwilling for personal or family reasons to jeopardize their jobs.

A slightly less common theme (7 of 26 relators) involved trying to prevent the fraudulent behavior from posing risks to public health. Most of the relators who described this type of motivation felt they had unique professional experiences or educational backgrounds that gave them a superior grasp of the negative public health implications of the illegal conduct. Some relators (7 of 26) characterized their action in reporting the fraud as emanating from a sense of duty to bring criminals to justice. Many of these relators were new employees who perceived themselves as being outside the fold in their companies.

Finally, several relators (5 of 26) reported fears that the fraudulent behavior would be discovered and would result in legal consequences for them; therefore, blowing the whistle was a way to protect themselves.

The Investigation. Whistle-blowers reported sharing several common experiences during the investigation phase of the litigation. First, most (15 of 26 relators, 14 of 22 insiders) became active players in the investigation. Their involvement included wearing a personal recording device at face-to-face meetings or national conferences, taping phone conversations with colleagues, and copying requested documents or files. In addition, after the Justice Department officially joined the case and began to obtain internal company documents by subpoena, relators were asked to work closely with department representatives to explain the evidence being gathered and help build the case.

Second, the workload and pressure were perceived as intense. One relator estimated spending "thousands of hours" on the case over its 5-year duration (Relator 17); another spent "probably 30 hours a week" during the first few years. Some meetings took place at Justice Department offices, with relators traveling at their own expense; others occurred unnervingly close to home. One reported that "a typical day could be meeting an FBI agent in a parkway rest stop. Sitting in his car with the windows rolled up. Neither heat nor air conditioning. Getting wired. Running to a meeting. . . . That might happen at 7 for a meeting at 8" (Relator 16). Another said, "I would have FBI agents show up in the office. I told them, the company people, that they were computer people. Luckily they believed it. . . . That's amusing now after the fact. But at the time they call you in 5 minutes. They say 'We're coming onto your campus'" (Relator 18).

Finally, there was widespread criticism of the Justice Department's collaborative posture, or lack thereof, during various phases of the investigation. Ten relators reported conflict with the investigators, most frequently at the outset. One remarked, "There was always an undertone of 'How much were we involved in this?'" (Relator 16). Relators also complained that "the government doesn't tell you anything" (Relator 5) about the status of the investigation, including when a settlement was imminent. Others were frustrated that "the wheels move really slow" and lamented the years spent waiting in a state of uncertainty (Relator 9).

Personal Toll. The experience of being involved in troubling corporate behavior and a qui tam case had substantial and long-lasting effects for nearly all of the insiders, although no similar problems were reported by any of the four outsiders. Eighteen insiders (82%) reported being subjected to various pressures by the company in response to their complaints (Table 3). A common theme was that the decision to blow the whistle had "put their career on the line" (Relator 3). For at least eight insiders, the financial consequences were reportedly devastating. One said, "I just wasn't able to get a job. It went longer and longer. Then I lost—I had a rental house that my kids were [using to go] to school. I had to sell the house. Then I had to sell the personal

Table 3. Forms of Pressure Reported by Insiders*

Type of Pressure	Illustrative Remark
Negative persuasion (reported by 7 relators)	"Then, after I complained, my territory changed. They started giving me more challenging physicians. Then they started giving me different areas farther out to call on. So it made it difficult to do my job." (Relator 15)
	"[N]obody spoke to me. Not one person. . . . I was persona non grata."(Relator 21)
Positive persuasion (reported by 4 relators)	"First, they attempted to promote me and bribe me to keep me quiet." (Relator 7)
	"I was contacted by their lawyers on a couple of different occasions. Including one time which was a random call. Somebody who was basically trying to ask me to drop the lawsuit. That I'd be given some money on the side." (Relator 9)
Direct intimidation (reported by 5 relators)	"The individuals that threatened me pointed out that the company would hang me out to dry and [said,] 'Even if they find something the company will throw you under the bus and prove that you were a loose cannon and the only person doing it.'" (Relator 25)
	"[They said] 'If you're not playing along with us the way we play, we'll throw you under the bus when and if anything ever hits the fan.'" (Relator 5)

* Insiders are whistle-blowers who were employees of the defendant company.

home that I was in. I had my cars repossessed. I just went—financially I went under. Then once you're financially under? Then no help. Then it really gets difficult. I lost my 401(k). I lost everything. Absolutely everything" (Relator 17).

Table 3 (continued)

Type of Pressure	Illustrative Remark
Loss of employment (reported by 5 relators)	Q: "Did you try to bring your concerns to your superiors?" A: "Yes." Q: "What happened then?" A: "I was fired." (Relator 9)
Blackballing (reported by 5 relators)	"Then I took a job. Then somehow [company name] called the job. Then I was fired." (Relator 8) "I had one interview with [company name] as national trainer. I was actually being offered the job. . . . [I was going to go] to the national meeting. Be introduced as the person in charge basically. I walked in to [the] vice president's office. They asked me to be escorted out of the room with security." (Relator 17)

Financial difficulties often were associated with personal problems. Six relators (all insiders) reported divorces, severe marital strain, or other family conflicts during this time. Thirteen relators reported having stress-related health problems, including shingles, psoriasis, autoimmune disorders, panic attacks, asthma, insomnia, temporomandibular joint disorder, migraine headaches, and generalized anxiety.

Settlement and Life Afterward. All relators in our sample received a share of the financial recovery. The amounts received ranged from $100,000 to $42 million, with a median of $3 million (net values, in 2009 dollars). The settlements helped alleviate some of the financial and nonfinancial costs of the litigation. One relator likened his large settlement to "hitting the lottery" (Relator 5). But a majority perceived their net recovery to be small relative to the time they spent on the case and the disruption and damage to their careers. After settlement, none of the 4 outsiders changed jobs, but only 2 of the 22 insiders remained employed in the pharmaceutical industry. One ruefully reported that he "should have taken the bribe" (Relator 7), and another noted that if she "stayed and took stock options" she "would've been worth a lot more" (Relator 4). The prevailing sentiment was that the payoff had not been worth the personal cost.

Despite the negative experiences and dissatisfaction with levels of financial recovery, 22 of the 26 relators still felt that what they did was important for ethical and other psychological or spiritual reasons. Relators offered a range of advice for others who might find themselves in similar situations (Table 4). Some offered strategic suggestions, such as hiring an experienced personal attorney, and many suggested a need to mentally prepare for a process more protracted, stressful, and conflict-ridden, and less financially rewarding, than prospective whistle-blowers might expect.

Policy Implications

This study identified several commonalities in whistle-blowers' experiences. Generally, whistle-blowers' first move was to try to address problems internally; they became litigators either accidentally (while pursuing other claims) or as a last resort. The most prevalent motivations reported were personal values and self-preservation rather than financial incentives. These findings provide a number of useful insights into the qui tam mechanism as a tool for addressing health care fraud.

First, the strain the process places on individuals' professional and personal lives may make prospective whistle-blowers

Table 4. Whistle-Blowers' Advice for Others Considering the Qui Tam Process

Topic of Advice	Illustrative Remark
Anticipated outcome	"I would say don't expect any money. It's going to be a long time. It's going to be frustrating. But if you're doing it for the right reasons? Then go for it. But if you're doing it because you think you're going to make millions? Don't do it." (Relator 9)
Relationship with government	"The government isn't there for you as much as you think. I really believe that. They're not there for you. They're ultimately there to get the company. You're just a tool. Just remember that you're just a tool for them." (Relator 8)
	"It wasn't overly friendly, it was just very methodical. It was very to the point. Very detailed, really. Very comprehensive." (Relator 13)
Investigation process	"The process is a long process." (Relator 4)
	"[Can they] afford 5 years of their life in turmoil? . . . If they [can't] I would tell them to find a new job and have a letter written anonymously with any documentation they can put together and send it off to the [Department of Justice]. Tell them to go investigate it. Or it's going to ruin their life." (Relator 7)
Evidentiary support	"Be as accurate as possible, have as much information as possible." (Relator 13)
	"Make sure you know really thoroughly, for sure, 200% certainty that what you think you know is accurate and factual." (Relator 19)

Table 4 (continued)

Topic of Advice	Illustrative Remark
Exhaust internal options	"[Bring a qui tam case] as an absolute last resort. Try and resolve it by changing things internally." (Relator 10)
	"Build alliances and arguments that demonstrate the value of correcting the wrong. . . . [Take] responsibility for becoming a catalyst for internal change. If you blow the whistle, regardless of your ethical foundation or ultimate success, your ability to live out your dreams is severely compromised." (Relator 25)
Sources of support	"You've got to find some people, because this could go on for a while, like a minister or a shrink who's confidentiality-protected. Part of your ability to do anything about this is keeping yourself together." (Relator 16)
	"You have to have strong resolve. Strong family life. To know what you want in life, if you want to risk things." (Relator 23)
Personal lawyers	"The first thing you need to do is get a good lawyer to represent you and guide you through this process because it's very complicated." (Relator 17)
	"[Find] somebody that has done it, somebody that has relationships, somebody that will be honest [and] prepare[d] to be involved." (Relator 14)
Deciding not to take action	"Don't do it. Either try to find another job or just shut your mouth and don't sign anything. They're going to keep doing it. So you're not going to make a change. It still goes on." (Relator 21)
	"Honestly, I would not advise anybody to do it." (Relator 6)

with legitimate evidence of fraud reluctant to come forward.[19] Social and medical complications related to the stress of involvement in litigation have been well documented in other legal contexts, such as malpractice,[20] where physicians may resort to extreme measures to avoid being sued.[21] Qui tam litigation, in contrast, involves a choice for those who initiate it. Its capacity to curb fraud may therefore be enhanced if Justice Department investigators and others involved in the process were more cognizant of the tribulations faced by relators, or if relators received needed resources (for example, temporary financial or medical benefits during unemployment) during the course of litigation. The long duration of the investigation process contributed to this stress. The reported backlog of nearly a thousand health care qui tam cases at the Justice Department suggests that this problem may get worse, not better, for relators in the foreseeable future.[22] Shortening the timelines and attendant stresses of qui tam litigation requires more resources for enforcement, an investment that should more than pay for itself.

Second, in many of the personal stories we heard, the financial recovery appeared to be quite disproportionate (in both positive and negative directions) to the whistle-blower's personal investment in the case. More sophisticated approaches to determining relators' recoveries could be used to promote both equity and more responsible whistle-blowing. For example, the FCA does not distinguish between relators outside and inside the defendant company, whereas we found that insiders tended to contribute much more to the Justice Department investigation

19. Devine T. The whistleblower's survival guide: courage without martyrdom. Washington, DC: Fund for Constitutional Government, 1997.

20. Charles S. Medical liability litigation as a disruptive life event. Bull Am Coll Surg 2005;90:17–23

21. Studdert DM, Mello MM, Sage WM, et al. Defensive medicine among high-risk specialist physicians in a volatile malpractice environment. JAMA 2005;293:2609–2617

22. Sen. Grassley: over 1,000 healthcare fraud cases await government action. Hospital Review. October 12, 2009. (Accessed April 22, 2010, at http://www.hospitalreviewmagazine .com/news-and-analysis/legal-and-regulatory/sen-grassley-over-1000-healthcare-fraud -cases-await-government-action.html.)

and suffered more for their involvement. Such factors should be taken into account in determining compensation.

Third, whereas retaliation is clearly proscribed by the FCA, our report suggests that the protections are not fully effective, particularly for insiders. Often, the retaliation was more subtle than overt harassment. For example, relators reported changes in employment duties that made meeting sales quotas or other expectations impossible, providing a pretext for job termination. For some relators, the anonymity gained from "sealing" their qui tam cases was undercut by the fact that internal complaints filed beforehand fingered them as obvious suspects. Ensuring responsible whistle-blowing in health care institutions may require broadening the scope, or strengthening the penalties, of the antiretaliation provisions.

This study has limitations. We focused on prosecutions against pharmaceutical companies that were taken up by the Justice Department and led to recoveries. Our findings may not be generalizable to other types of qui tam litigation, and the experiences of relators in our sample may be more positive, on average, than those of whistle-blowers whose cases were not successful. Our findings represent the subjective experiences that whistle-blowers were willing to report in interviews. Responses to some queries, such as motivations and the role played by the prospect of financial gain, may reflect a socially desirable response bias. Finally, responses may be subject to recall bias. Notwithstanding these limitations, our findings suggest that changes to the FCA and qui tam process that mitigate relators' hardships may help promote responsible whistle-blowing and enhance the effectiveness of this integral component of efforts to combat health care fraud.

> *"The line separating an unethical snitch or nark and a whistleblower is thin and often blurry."*

Whistleblowers May Have Moral and Immoral Motivations

Matthias Kleinhempel

Matthias Kleinhempel is the director of the Center for Governance and Transparency at IAE Business School in Buenos Aires. In the following viewpoint, he argues that whistleblowing can be seen as an ethical act or as a betrayal of loyalty. He says the ethical status of whistleblowing depends in part on the whistleblower's motivations. These, he says, can range from a desire to right a wrong, to the desire for financial gain from government, to the desire for revenge. Kleinhempel concludes that many companies are moving to reward whistleblowers themselves, giving whistleblowers an incentive to keep their findings internal rather than going to the government.

As you read, consider the following questions:

1. What is "rational loyalty" according to Kleinhempel?

2. When was the Dodd-Frank Act passed and what effect does Kleinhempel say it may have toward corporate responses to whistleblowing?
3. What consequences does Kleinhempel say whistleblowers may face?

Historically, whistleblowing has been viewed as contrary to organizations' interests. Ethics scholars argued that whistleblowing went against loyalty to an organization, with sayings like "don't wash your dirty laundry in public" supporting this notion among the general public. Whistleblowing brought back memories of informers in countries with totalitarian episodes in their past, like Nazi Germany, Eastern Germany, the USSR, etc.

Snitches vs. Whistleblowers

The line separating an unethical snitch or nark and a whistleblower is thin and often blurry. The main distinction lies in the deed revealed and the whistleblower's motivation. The question is whether hiding a misconduct in the rule of law is more adequate than its exposure. Reporting any wrongdoing—at least internally—affords an organization the possibility to take remedial steps or, at least, mitigate potential consequences. Public exposure comes as a result of a simple fact: the members of an organization are necessarily also members of a larger organization—society at large. Disclosing illegal activities may be necessary, and it amounts to an act of loyalty to society as a whole.

The meaning of "loyalty towards an organization" should be defined more clearly. Several authors have coined and explained the notion of "rational loyalty." This type of faithfulness does not lie with an organization's top management and its employees, but with the company's mission, code of conduct, and goals.

Organizations announcing their mission, values, and code of conduct on brochures, annual reports, and websites explicitly indicate that their efforts are geared towards accomplishing the values stated. They seek to persuade their shareholders and other stakeholders about the alignment between what they proclaim and what they do. If adhering to these statements is an act of loyalty, then whistleblowers are faithful to their organizations when they reveal any wrongdoing that goes against their organizations' code of conduct, values, and mission. In a nutshell, loyalty lies not with a group of individuals but with the organization at large.

Nonetheless, this will hardly bring discussions on whistleblowing ethics to an end. Ultimately, several values and criteria may be aligned or at odds. To weigh these values and criteria appropriately, this analysis should encompass not only faithfulness towards the organization, but also the materiality of the disclosed deed and its veracity, whether it is an internal or external disclosure, and the motivations driving the whistleblower to report such act.

Altruism, Money, or Revenge

Regarding the materiality criterion and the certainty that the wrongdoing has actually happened and can be proved, the matter is relatively simple: the more relevant and truthful the deed, the more justified the whistleblowing. The purest, loftiest motivation for whistleblowing is altruistic: the whistleblower reports a misconduct to remedy a wrongdoing, to avoid or repair the damage made to the organization, its employees or customers—and, by extension, to society at large. Regardless of this selfless motivation, whistleblowing can sometimes bring significant financial gain for whistleblowers. In the US, the False Claims Act provides monetary incentives for whistleblowers, which were expanded by the Dodd-Frank Act in 2011. In turn, companies themselves offer rewards to whistleblowers. Indeed, corporate incentives are likely to spread and rise in the future to discourage potential whistleblowers from choosing to make their disclosures public in order to seize the rewards set forth by the Dodd-Frank Act, instead of reporting them internally and giving their organizations the opportunity to take remedial steps and to avert public exposure.

Yet, not every motivation that is not altruistic is necessarily financial. Revenge or blackmail—to get a promotion or any other workplace-related benefit—and even the fear to lose one's job—if a wrongdoing is disclosed externally and the organization succumbs to a scandal—are also strong drivers for whistleblowers. At one extreme, external, direct whistleblowing (with no prior internal tip) on an issue that is not material for the organization and fueled by a vengeful desire or economic gain does seem like a disloyal, unethical act. The opposing extreme case would involve reporting on a serious misconduct, like an act of corruption, to top management to prevent it or to mitigate the damage to the organization. Most whistleblowing incidents fall within a scope that spans between these two extremes. Ultimately, every individual will need to make conscientious assessment of the criteria mentioned above to make the right decision.

Most often, individuals choose to blow the whistle when organizations around them favor a culture of transparency, with open-door policies and procedures in place to protect whistleblowers. Research has shown that employees feel more inclined to report wrongdoings when they are pleased with their companies and believe management is fully committed to ethical values. Attitudes may change as a result of management behavior and according to personal standards, also shaped by external factors, such as local culture and beliefs. Some individuals require more support than others; some are driven by monetary incentives, while others are more concerned with justice or decide to blow the whistle if they have a user-friendly, convenient tool to do so. The most common motivation not to report a misconduct is a belief that the organization will fail to take any corrective measures and that details will not remain confidential, threatening whistleblowers' professional and personal lives.

Betrayal or Benefit

Whistleblowing does not only entail an ethical dilemma, but also a question as to whether reporting a specific wrongdoing accounts for a betrayal or a benefit for the organization and society. This complex quandary often brings severe consequences for whistleblowers. As a result of a tip or report, the organization may choose to investigate the events involved and may come to a decision based on its findings. Yet, it is also possible that nothing happens—that is, the organization and the people handling the report may choose to ignore it. To make matters worse, in several cases, organizations have not only ignored the report but also punished whistleblowers, who have been viewed as a threat to their co-workers, superiors, and top management. Whistleblowers may end up losing their jobs, being denied salary raises, risking social isolation, etc. Oftentimes, whistleblowers are forced to change jobs—and even countries. It may even be hard for them to find new employment: companies do not want to hire whistleblowers, who are often portrayed as "troublemakers," while colleagues just shun them, for fear of becoming the next "victim" of a report. Retaliation to whistleblowers is common around the world and takes many subtle and drastic forms. However, this phenomenon is slowly changing, primarily as a result of two major drivers: On the one hand, retaliation involves a risk for the organization. When companies provide protection to whistleblowers—eventually even rewarding them financially, whistleblowing tends to take place and remain inside the company. Instead, when whistleblowers do not expect a favorable response from the organization, they tend to seek an external means to disclose a misconduct, with strong incentives offered by current laws, like the Dodd-Frank Act, and associated costs for other parties involved.

On the other hand, companies are increasingly realizing that transparency and good business practices both provide sound competitive advantages and minimize public exposure risks—as well as their associated costs. Either from ethical convictions, to gain an edge over competitors or to avert risks, corporate behavior is changing. Business organizations are rolling out compliance programs with specific rules to protect whistleblowers from any form of retaliation.

> "[Phaedra Almajid] admitted that the false accusations were an act of revenge after she was axed from the Qatar 2022 bid campaign."

Whistleblowers May Be Motivated by Revenge to Make False Accusations

Mark Bisson

Mark Bisson is an Olympics and football (soccer) business journalist who writes for World Football INSIDER *and AroundThe Rings.com. In the following viewpoint, he reports on an instance in which a whistleblower was motivated by revenge to make false accusations. Phaedra Almajid was working on Qatar's bid to host the World Cup. When Qatar ended her employment, she became angry, Bisson reports, and accused Qatar of bribing World Cup officials. The whistleblowing accusations received worldwide attention. Bisson reports that Almajid finally withdrew her accusations, admitting she had lied.*

As you read, consider the following questions:

1. How much did the whistleblower claim Qatar officials paid to the FIFA commission, according to Bisson?

2. In what large newspapers were Almajid's claims published, according to the viewpoint?

3. What other accusations of bribery involving FIFA does Bisson discuss?

FIFA [Fédération Internationale de Football Association] confirms it has received an email from the whistleblower who alleged the Qatar 2022 World Cup [the international soccer championship] bid paid $1.5 million to three FIFA members in which she admits to lying about the claims.

Bribery Allegations

Phaedra Almajid, a press officer for the Gulf state's bid, had said that Confederation of African Football president Issa Hayatou, Ivory Coast football leader Jacques Anouma and Nigeria's suspended FIFA Ex-Co member Amos Adamu were paid bribes to vote for Qatar.

She admitted that the false accusations were an act of revenge after she was axed from the Qatar 2022 bid campaign.

FIFA today said it was not making any specific comment on the retraction of the allegations and pointed to its May 30 [2011] statement that said world football's [that is, soccer's] governing body had not received "any evidence whatsoever" from the *Sunday Times* or from the whistleblower with regard to allegations made against Hayatou and Anouma.

"In a consistent and correct way, we have repeatedly said that FIFA would not be making any comments on allegations. This policy will continue," today's FIFA statement said.

"In a consistent and correct way, we have repeatedly said that FIFA can only act upon evidence. This policy will continue. When only allegations are made and no evidence is given, FIFA always stands firmly by its members."

Almajid's original allegations first surfaced in a written submission from a *Sunday Times* investigation into FIFA bribery claims that went before a British parliamentary inquiry in May. All three FIFA EX-Co members denied any wrongdoing.

At the time, the Qatar Football Association said the submission contained "a series of serious, unsubstantiated, and false allegations regarding the conduct of the bid committee."

Al Majid was invited by FIFA president Sepp Blatter to back up her claims but she never showed up for talks.

INSIDER has seen Almajid's letter and sworn affidavit retracting the allegations that was sent to FIFA, the Asian Football Confederation, Qatar 2022 bid, and Confederation of African Football as well as those she accused of bribery.

The Qatar Whistleblower

She reveals that her revenge mission on Qatar 2022 began when she left the bid after being informed that officials were looking to replace her.

"I was hurt and very bitter," she said. "I wanted to hurt the bid like they had hurt me. I also wanted to show them that I could control the international media and started speaking with the journalists about Qatar, and became the "Qatar Whistleblower".

"The whistleblower stories were then published in the biggest newspapers in US and England—the *Wall Street Journal* and the *Sunday Times*—showing that I did understand the media. Things were becoming too serious though, and the story became much bigger and more high profile than I thought it would."

In her letter to Qatar 2022 World Cup organisers, Issa Hayatou, Jacques Anouma, Amos Adamu and FIFA, she apologised for the "fabricated allegations".

"I have lied about all facts concerning the behaviour and practice of the Qatar 2022 bid," she said.

"Never, at any time, were any bribes even offered, suggested or paid on behalf of the Qatar 2022 bid during any time in exchange for votes from Issa Hayatou, Jacques Anouma, and Amos Adamu.

"Never at any time did I wish, nor did I foresee, the extent in which these lies would be projected by the international media

—even to the extent that they were presented to the United Kingdom's Parliamentary Select Committee Inquiry into Football Governance.

"I am very sorry for any and all embarrassment caused to the various individuals and authorities concerned.

"I was very proud to work on behalf of the Qatar 2022 bid committee and have no doubt that the country will stage an outstanding, ground-breaking, and highly successful World Cup.

She added: "I also wish to state that the decision to make this admission is entirely my own: I have not been subject to any form of pressure or been offered any financial inducement to do so."

Notwithstanding the retraction of allegations, the bribery allegations swirling around FIFA are expected to generate more negative headlines for football's governing body over the coming months.

Mohamed Bin Hammam, the suspended Asian football boss who is accused of buying Caribbean Football Union [CFU] votes in his bid to unseat Sepp Blatter, is scheduled to attend a FIFA ethics committee hearing on July 22.

The Qatari is accused of colluding with former FIFA vice president Jack Warner to pay $40,000 cash bribes to 25 CFU members at a meeting in May in exchange for votes for him.

FIFA will deliver its verdict on July 23. A leaked ethics committee report cited "overwhelming evidence" against the pair. Both deny any wrongdoing.

If he is sanctioned, Bin Hammam is expected to appeal, dragging the bribery case out until the end of the year through the Court of Arbitration for Sport.

> "Qui tam laws provide an incentive to corporate insiders who are in the best position to learn of frauds and other misconduct for which a qui tam reward may be available."

Rewards Give Whistleblowers a Motivation to Reveal Wrongdoing

Stephen Martin Kohn

Stephen M. Kohn is an attorney for Kohn, Kohn & Colapinto, a law firm specializing in employment law. In the following viewpoint, he argues that corporate fraud cannot be exposed without the help of whistleblowers. Therefore, he argues, it is vital to encourage whistleblowers to come forward to expose wrongdoing. He says that qui tam laws that give whistleblowers a financial reward provide an important incentive. He concludes that qui tam laws providing rewards for whistleblowers are an important tool to help catch corporate criminals.

As you read, consider the following questions:

1. According to Kohn, what did whistleblowers find wrong with Eli Lilly and Company's practices?

2. What does Kohn say inspired the original legislation that became the False Claims Act?

3. What mandatory guidelines did the 1986 amendments to the False Claims Act set for whistleblower compensation, according to Kohn?

The single most important rule for whistleblowers is very simple: Follow the money. Four major federal laws provide for the payment of rewards to whistleblowers who can prove that their employers committed fraud. These rewards can be large. Between 1987 and 2010 the federal government paid out to whistleblowers over $2.877 billion in compensation. The laws are based on a medieval concept known as *qui tam*, that translates from its Latin roots as "he who brings a case on behalf of our lord King, as well as for himself." Under *qui tam* citizens are encouraged to help the government enforce the law "in the name of the King." The principle behind *qui tam* is simple: If your disclosure results in the recovery of money for the "King," you obtain a portion of the monies recovered. . . .

The critical role *qui tam* laws play in stopping fraud was explained in the 2008 Senate Judiciary Committee Report on the FCA [False Claims Act]. Quoting from University of Alabama Bainbridge Professor of Law Pamela Bucy's testimony, the committee concluded:

> Complex economic wrongdoing cannot be detected or deterred effectively without the help of those who are intimately familiar with it. Law enforcement will always be outsiders to organizations where fraud is occurring. They will not find out about such fraud until it is too late, if at all. . . . Given these facts, insiders who are willing to blow the whistle are the only effective way to learn that wrongdoing has occurred.

Qui tam laws provide an incentive to corporate insiders who are in the best position to learn of frauds and other misconduct for which a *qui tam* reward may be available. They are the only whistleblower laws that both provide on-the-job protection against retaliation and incentives to encourage employees to undertake enormous personal risks.

The False Claims Act

The oldest *qui tam* law, the False Claims Act, was originally enacted in 1863 but was amended in 1943 and 1986. The law was further strengthened by three additional amendments signed into law in 2009 and 2010. Since being modernized in 1986, it has proven to be the most effective antifraud law in the United States (and perhaps the entire world).

How do you know if your disclosures impact the FCA? Ask yourself the following question: Is the taxpayer on the hook for any of the costs that may be incurred for any employer misconduct you have identified? If government funds are involved, the worker who exposes fraud against the taxpayer may find him- or herself covered under this most powerful whistleblower law. The FCA has actually made millionaires out of ordinary workers who did the "right thing." It provides large financial incentives to employees who demand that their companies engage in honest and ethical practices—and who turn them in when they don't stop cheating.

The reasoning behind the law is simple: Reward people for doing the right thing. Under the FCA's *qui tam* procedures, for every dollar the government collects from contractors who abused the system, the whistleblower obtains a reward set at between 15 percent and 30 percent of the monies collected. In an age of multibillion dollar stimulus spending, bulging federal health care costs and massive defense contracting, the reach of programs or companies obtaining taxpayer monies is staggering.

To understand the importance of the FCA, the recent experiences of the powerful drug company Eli Lilly and Company are illuminating. In January 2009 Lilly agreed to pay $1.4 billion in fines and penalties. Whistleblowers caught this company illegally marketing the drug Zyprexa. To increase sales the company minimized health risks associated with the drug. As it turns out the taxpayer was a big victim of Lilly's illegal marketing schemes. Doctors were sold on writing prescriptions for Zyprexa. Patients were sold on buying Zyprexa. But the bills were sent to the taxpayer, courtesy of the gigantic Medicare and Medicaid programs. Whistleblowers who worked for Eli Lilly knew of the company's illegal marketing scheme, knew of the problems associated with the drug, and knew of the potential adverse medical effects. They also knew that taxpayers were paying the bill for the illegal marketing scheme while the company made billions in profits improperly selling Zyprexa.

Under the FCA these Eli Lilly whistleblowers were empowered to directly sue the company. Their lawsuit triggered a Justice Department investigation into the company's wrongdoing. In the Lilly case the investigation resulted in a massive settlement. The company was forced to pay $800 million to the federal and state governments to reimburse the Medicare and Medicaid programs. The company had to pay an additional $615 million in criminal penalties. The whistleblowers used the FCA as a vehicle for a systemic nationwide investigation into illegal drug-marketing practices. The company got caught, and the law forced Eli Lilly to pay the penalty. Thus the big winners were the taxpayers and the safety of all.

Everyday workers had forced one of the world's most powerful drug companies to pay $1.1 billion from its illegal profits back to the American taxpayer. Additionally, the workers who risked their careers to serve the public interest obtained a "whistleblower reward" of over $78.87 million. The nine whistleblowers involved in the case were rewarded for doing the right thing, risking their jobs and careers, and serving the public interest. In the end, they were not the stereotypical whistleblower-martyr. They were the victors.

The Eli Lilly workers followed the first rule for whistleblowers. They followed the money by tracking who profited and who paid. By following the money, they found the best law that would protect and reward their whistleblowing.

The Birth of Modern Whistleblower Protections

To understand how the False Claims Act (and the other *qui tam* laws) works, it is critical to understand the history behind the FCA. The law was 125 years in the making. The current complex requirements of the law reflect its birth in 1863, during the height of the Civil War, and two sweeping amendments in 1943 and 1986.

During the Civil War, President [Abraham] Lincoln and his supporters in Congress were disgusted with government contractors, some of whom were selling sawdust as gunpowder and profiting from the terrible costs of the war. Congressional investigations uncovered "waste and squandering" of "public funds." Overcharging was common, and war contracts were given "without any advertising" at "exorbitant rates above market value."

When Congress investigated the frauds, it discovered that insider employees had blown the whistle and were subjected to retaliation. In one case the employee architect of the Benton barracks in Missouri reported that he was "cursed and abused," "terrified," and threatened with imprisonment for blowing the whistle on bribes paid to obtain construction contracts for the barracks.

To encourage citizens to disclose these frauds, Senator Jacob Howard from Michigan introduced into Congress bill number S. 467, what is today referred to as the False Claims Act. As Senator Howard explained, a key provision in the law was a "*qui tam* clause" "based" on the "old-fashioned idea of holding out a temptation" for persons to step forward and turn in thieves. Howard understood that this *qui tam* mechanism would empower citizens to sue wrongdoers in the name of the United States Government (i.e., "in the name of the King") in order to ensure compliance with the law. Senator Howard strongly defended the *qui tam* provisions in the bill as in his words, the "safest and most expeditious way I have ever discovered of bringing rogues to justice."

Under the original law, any person who had knowledge of the fraud—referred to today as "whistleblowers"—were authorized to file a lawsuit on behalf of the United States. If frauds were proven, the wrongdoer had to pay up twice the amount of the fraud, plus a large fine of $2,000. The whistleblower, known in the law as the "relator," would get half the money, and the United States would collect the other half.

On March 2, 1863, President Lincoln started the ball rolling when he signed into law S. 467, a "bill to prevent and punish frauds upon the Government of the United States." The FCA was visionary legislation. It was passed before the rise of modern industry and before the federal government became a multitrillion-dollar enterprise. Like other visionary civil rights legislation signed into law during the Civil War and Reconstruction, it was progressive, years ahead of its time; its use would remain dormant until the New Deal and the outbreak of World War II, when government procurement would reach a previously unimaginable amount.

In the early 1940s, in the wake of large war-related federal spending, the FCA was dusted off and a handful of *qui tam* suits were filed. By 1943 a mere twenty-eight FCA cases were pending in all the courts in the United States. Although small in number, they targeted some of the most powerful corporations and political machines in the country, including Carnegie-Illinois Steel Corporation (for selling "substandard" steel to the Navy); the Anaconda Wire & Cable Company (for selling "defective wire and cable"); contracts awarded to Hague Machine (led by Frank Hague, Jersey City mayor and the co-chair of the Democratic National Committee); and corrupt contracts awarded to a company owned by Tom Prendergast, the notorious "boss" from Kansas City.

These suits caused panic within the powerful government-contractor community. Before the law was ever really tested, Congress voted to gut out the heart of the FCA. . . .

After 1943, attempts by whistleblowers to use the FCA were fruitless. *Qui tam* relators or whistleblowers could not get around the numerous procedural or substantive roadblocks that prevented them from filing claims or collecting recoveries. Consequently, over one hundred attempts to use the law to hold contractors accountable failed in the courts. The law was down and out, but not dead.

Resurrection and the False Claims Reform Act

At the height of the "[President Ronald] Reagan Revolution," [during the 1980s] and its gargantuan increases in defense spending, a freshman senator from Iowa, Senator Chuck Grassley, led the charge to increase oversight and accountability for federal spending by resurrecting the False Claims Act. In 1985 he, along with Congressman Howard Berman, introduced the False Claims Reform Act.

The Senate Judiciary Committee held hearings on the Reform Amendment. The record before the committee was shocking—since 1943 contractor abuses had gotten completely out of control. In fact, things were so bad that the General Accounting Office reached the following conclusion after carefully studying government fraud: "The sad truth is that crime against the Government often *does* pay."

In the middle of the Congressional debate over the Reform Amendment, new scandals rocked the contractor world. When members of Congress took to the floor and exposed that contractors had billed the taxpayers $7,622 for a coffee pot, $435 for a hammer, and $640 for a toilet seat, the media responded. These outrageous examples of contractor abuse outraged the public and generated strong support in Congress for the reforms. On October 27, 1986, the False Claims Reform Act was overwhelmingly passed by Congress and signed into law by President Ronald Reagan.

The 1986 False Claims Act Amendments

The False Claims Reform Act reversed the most vicious anti-whistleblower provisions of the 1943 amendments, modernized the law, restored the rights of whistleblowers to file claims, and set mandatory reward levels, regardless of the amount of money collected from the corrupt or abusive contractor.

The 1986 amendments reestablished the rights of whistle-blowers to file *qui tam* lawsuits. It permitted whistleblowers to directly litigate their cases against contractors, whether or not the United States joined in the action. In other words, if the United States decided not to file any claim against the contractor, the whistleblower had the right to continue the lawsuit on his or her own, conduct discovery, participate in a trial, and attempt to prove that the contractor had stolen from the taxpayer. If the United States decided to join the lawsuit, the whistleblower was still guaranteed the right to participate in the case, protect his or her rights, and present the case against the contractor.

The 1986 amendments also set mandatory guidelines for monetarily rewarding whistleblowers. If a whistleblower filed a FCA suit and the United States used this information to collect damages from the contractor, the whistleblower was guaranteed between 15 percent and 25 percent of the total monies collected. If the government refused to hold the contractor accountable, the whistleblower could pursue the case "in the name of the United States," even without the intervention or support of the Justice Department. If the whistleblower won the claim, he or she would be entitled to between 20 percent and 30 percent of the amount of money collected by the United States. These provisions held, and the Justice Department did not have the authority or discretion to reduce whistleblower rewards below the statutory minimums.

Other provisions of the law were substantially improved as well. First, Congress no longer simply doubled the amount of money owed by the contractor. The law called for treble damages —the contractor would have to pay three times the amount of the fraud. Second, the amount of the per-violation fine was increased from $2,000 to between $5,000 and $10,000. The contractor would have to pay the attorney fees and costs incurred by the whistleblower in pursing the claim. An antiretaliation provision was also included in the law. Companies were prohibited from firing or discriminating against employees who filed FCA lawsuits. A worker could file a multimillion-dollar claim against his company and the company was strictly prohibited from firing the employee. If fired, the employee was entitled to reinstatement and double back pay, along with traditional special damages, and attorney fees and costs. . . .

Taxes, Securities, and Commodities

The False Claims Act has worked. Between 1986 and 2010, under this law well over $27 billion was paid back into the U.S. Treasury. Countless billions of dollars were saved through better regulations and internal corporate oversight sparked by the fear of FCA cases. During this time period whistleblowers obtained $2.877 billion in payouts. It was becoming cost-effective to follow the law.

Based on these successes, Congress enacted three new *qui tam* laws, covering taxes (2006), securities fraud (2010), and fraud in the commodities futures market (2010). Each of the laws is somewhat different, but given the breadth of coverage, numerous whistleblowers will be covered under their provisions. Taxpayers, honest investors, and contractors who play by the rules will be the winners.

For example, the ink was hardly dry on the federal tax whistleblower law before billions of dollars in claims were filed with the IRS [Internal Revenue Service]. Most famous of these were allegations submitted by Bradley Birkenfeld, a banker who had

Unofficial US Justice Department Overview of Whistleblower Law

The False Claims Act, 31 U.S.C. § 3729 et seq., provides for liability for triple damages and a penalty from $5,500 to $11,000 per claim for anyone who knowingly submits or causes the submission of a false or fraudulent claim to the United States.

The statute, first passed in 1863, includes an ancient legal device called a "qui tam" provision (from a Latin phrase meaning "he who brings a case on behalf of our lord the King, as well as for himself"). This provision allows a private person, known as a "relator," to bring a lawsuit on behalf of the United States, where the private person has information that the named defendant has knowingly submitted or caused the submission of false or fraudulent claims to the United States. The relator need not have been personally harmed by the defendant's conduct.

The False Claims Act has a very detailed process for the filing and pursuit of these claims. The qui tam relator must be represented by an attorney. The qui tam complaint must, by law, be filed under seal, which means that all records relating to the case must be kept on a secret docket by the Clerk of the Court. Copies of the complaint are given only to the United States Department of Justice, including the local United States Attorney, and to the assigned judge of the District Court. The Court may, usually upon motion by the United States Attorney, make the complaint available to other persons.

Justice Department, False Claim Act
Cases: Government Intervention in Qui Tam
(Whistleblower) Suits. *www.justice.gov.*

worked for UBS bank in Switzerland. When Birkenfeld blew the whistle, UBS was the largest bank in the world. It had created a "major wealth" section that catered to offshore North American accounts. Over nineteen thousand Americans had stashed their wealth into this UBS program, where their income was hidden and taxes were evaded. Because the accounts were "secret," the stock trades conducted on behalf of these millionaires and billionaires by the UBS bankers were all illegal. The North American program had $20 billion in assets, all in secret "non-disclosed" accounts that violated numerous U.S. tax laws.

Within months of the passage of the new IRS whistleblower law, Birkenfeld walked into the offices of the Department of Justice with thousands of pages of evidence fully documenting the UBS tax scheme. He provided all the details of the accounts, including the fact that the UBS bankers regularly traveled to the United States with encrypted laptops to transact illegal business with their American clients. The scandal that followed shook UBS and Swiss banking to its core.

When the Justice Department confronted UBS with Birkenfeld's information, the bank immediately folded its hand and paid up. UBS agreed to a $780 million settlement with the United States. Moreover, they agreed, for the first time in Swiss history, to turn over the names of more than four thousand U.S. citizens who held illegal accounts with the bank.

Thousands of Americans with Swiss accounts feared being exposed to public shame, heavy fines, and criminal prosecutions. The IRS capitalized on these fears and initiated a one-time "amnesty program," in which U.S. citizens with illegal offshore accounts could confidentially turn themselves in, pay reasonable penalties, and escape criminal prosecution. Over fourteen thousand Americans took advantage of this program and paid the U.S. Treasury fines and penalties estimated at over $5 billion.

What was the role of the whistleblower in the largest ever tax fraud case? That was the very question asked by the federal judge to the prosecutor in the Birkenfeld case:

The Court: Now, you said something that has great significance . . . but for Mr. Birkenfeld this scheme would still be ongoing?

The Prosecutor: I have no reason to believe that we would have had any other means to have disclosed what was going on but for an insider in that scheme providing detailed information, which Mr. Birkenfeld did.

The legendary system of Swiss bank secrecy was cracked wide open by *one* former employee turned whistleblower. *One* whistleblower forced the largest Swiss bank to shut down a $20 billion, highly profitable program and pay the U.S. Treasury a large fine. *One* whistleblower's disclosure triggered widespread voluntary compliance with the tax laws, resulting in additional billions of dollars pouring into the U.S. Treasury. The first publicly known case under the 2006 IRS whistleblower law resulted in the largest tax fraud recoveries in U.S. history. *Qui tam* laws work.

> "These data suggest that although
> rewards under existing whistleblower
> programs may be substantial, general
> use of the programs is not high."

Reward Programs Do Not Motivate Whistleblowers

Jonathan L. Awner and Denise Dickins

Jonathan L. Awner is the chairman of the national corporate practice group at the law firm Akerman Senterfitt; Denise Dickins is assistant professor of accounting and auditing at East Carolina University. In the following viewpoint, they argue that the number of whistleblowers who get federal bounties is low. The federal whistleblowing programs, the authors say, are not well advertised and are underfunded. New whistleblowing programs, they say are also unlikely to be heavily used. The authors conclude that this is just as well, since it suggests there will be few instances in which whistleblowers make false accusations in order to reap bounties.

As you read, consider the following questions:

1. What protections for whistleblowers are included in Dodd-Frank, according to the authors of this viewpoint?

2. Why does the IRS say it should not have to pay a bounty to the employee of Switzerland-based UBS despite the fact that he blew the whistle on wrongdoing, according to the authors?

3. Why do the authors say that firm-sponsored bounties to encourage whistleblowers are not necessary?

On July 21, 2010, President [Barack] Obama signed into law the Dodd-Frank Wall Street Reform and Consumer Protection Act. Critics decried the legislation as one of the most onerous pieces of corporate governance regulation since the Sarbanes-Oxley Act of 2002 (SOX).

Encouraging Whistleblowers

One of Dodd-Frank's most contentious provisions is Section 922, which directs the Securities and Exchange Commission [SEC] to implement a "whistleblower" program by which individuals may report suspected securities violations to the agency. Previously, SOX's Section 301 had required firms' audit committees to establish and monitor whistleblower programs by which suspected violations could be reported internally, but Dodd-Frank elevates whistleblowing by enabling employees, vendors, and customers, among others, to bypass companies' internal control systems and report accusations directly to the U.S. Government. Dodd-Frank further stipulates that whistleblowers could receive as much as 30 percent of any fines, penalties, or the repayment of losses resulting from their reports.

Firms, attorneys, and others have been vocal about the potential for harm associated with the Dodd-Frank whistleblowing mechanisms. The SEC received over 950 comment letters following its publication of proposed rules for implementing Section 922. In particular, concerns have been expressed about the potential for disgruntled individuals to make unsubstantiated accusations in an effort to gain financial rewards, and the potential adverse impact of false claims on stock prices and customer and vendor relationships.

In this article, we attempt to determine how heavily the Dodd-Frank whistleblower bounty program might be utilized and the likelihood that it would be successful in its mission to "encourage people to report securities violations." We do this by examining two analogous federal bounty programs, the Federal False Claims Act of 1863, as amended in 1986 and 2008, and the Internal Revenue Service's [IRS's] Informant Claims Program. Our results suggest that, although rewards under these programs may be substantial, general use of the programs is not high. In light of Dodd-Frank's similarities to these programs, and an expected lack of adequate federal funding to pursue reported claims, it is likely Section 922 will have similar results.

Comparing Whistleblower Programs

The United States has used whistleblower programs for almost 150 years. Below is a brief description of three of these programs, along with the Section 922 program.

The FFCA. The Federal False Claims Act (FFCA) offers incentives to individuals who report companies or individuals defrauding the government. It was implemented by President [Abraham] Lincoln in 1863 to protect the United States from purchases of fake gunpowder during the Civil War. Claims under the FFCA are typically related to health care or the military, and often report over-billing or billing for fraudulent services. Reporting of suspected tax fraud is excluded under the FFCA and instead is covered by the IRS's whistleblower program described below.

As amended in 1986 and 2009, the FFCA offers financial incentives to whistleblowers of up to 30 percent of any recovery. It also includes anti-retaliation provisions including reinstatement, damages, and double back pay for workers who report their employers. Claims under the FFCA are filed with the Department of Justice under seal, meaning they will not be made public until the government decides to intervene. Claims cannot be brought against members of the armed forces, the judiciary, Congress, or senior executive branch officials.

To reduce the likelihood of false accusations, the FFCA imposes monetary penalties on individuals reporting false claims. Some states have enacted laws similar to the FFCA.

ICP. The Informant Claims Program (ICP), implemented under Section 7623 of the Internal Revenue Code, has been in effect since 1867. Under the ICP, an individual may report a taxpayer who underreports his tax liabilities, and the whistleblower could receive a bounty in return for the report.

The ICP's only substantial modification came in 2006 when discretion of the amount of bounty paid to whistleblowers was removed, eligibility thresholds were enacted, and whistleblower appeals were provided. Under the program's current form, if the IRS successfully uses the whistleblower's information against an individual with adjusted gross income of at least $200,000 or an entity with underpayments of at least $2 million, the whistleblower is entitled to a bounty of up to 30 percent of funds collected, including taxes, penalties, and interest. Whistleblower bounties of up to 15 percent of recovered amounts are also available for smaller disputes. The IRS reserves the right to refuse payment of a bounty if the whistleblower is convicted of criminal conduct associated with the reported tax evasion.

SOX. The [2002] Sarbanes-Oxley Act's [SOX] Section 301 requires issuers' audit committees to implement mechanisms for recording, tracking, and acting on information about potential securities violations provided by employees anonymously and confidentially. SOX Section 806 also broadened previous whistleblower protections to cover employees who report fraud to any federal regulatory or law enforcement agency, any member or committee of Congress, or any person with supervisory authority over the employee. Potential securities violations reported to a federal agency or an internal corporate compliance office under SOX carry no opportunity for financial bounty.

Dodd-Frank. To be eligible for a bounty under the Dodd-Frank Act's Section 922, individuals—not organizations—must submit original information derived from the whistleblower's independent knowledge pertaining to a corporation's violation of securities laws. If the information results in a recovery, including fines and penalties, of at least $1 million from the accused corporation, the whistleblower may earn a bounty of 10–30 percent of the recovery. For example, if an employee supplies the SEC with a duplicate set of financial records that suggests his or her employer has reported falsified financial information and, as a result of the SEC's investigation, the corporation is required to pay a $ 1 million fine, the whistleblower is eligible for a bounty of up to $300,000.

Individuals who are convicted of a crime related to the reported misconduct or who participate in reported violations are not eligible for the bounty. For example, if an employee of a foreign, government-controlled entity reports evidence of receiving a $10,000 bribe from a U.S. corporation to secure a $5 million contract and, as a result of the SEC's investigation, the corporation must pay a $10 million fine under the Foreign Corrupt Practices Act, the reporting individual would not be eligible for a bounty. Issuers' internal compliance personnel, attorneys, auditors, and other recipients of privileged communications are also ineligible to receive bounties for claims related to their clients' securities violations. Uncertainty as to how the SEC would treat a whistleblower under these proposed disqualification rules may discourage whistleblowers from filing claims.

Dodd-Frank also includes protections for the whistleblower against employer retaliation. In the event of successful claims, protections include the possibility of reinstatement, double back pay with interest, expert witness fees, and attorney fees.

Whistleblowers and the Federal False Claims Act (FFCA)

Year	Settlements and judgments (in millions)	Bounties (in millions)	Number of new whistleblower reports
2001	$1,838.00	$218.10	311
2002	1,223.50	166.00	318
2003	2,247.50	338.60	334
2004	685.90	112.50	432
2005	1,433.40	170.60	406
5-year average	1,485.66	201.16	360
2006	3,222.90	225.40	384
2007	2,050.50	191.30	365
2008	1,364.00	202.30	379
2009	2,457.60	258.80	433
2010	3,012.30	385.20	573
5-year average	2,421.46	252.60	427
Difference in 5-year periods	635.80	51.44	67

TAKEN FROM: Jonathan L. Awner and Denise Dickens, "Will There Be Whistleblowers?," *Cato Foundation*, Summer 2011, pp. 36–39. www.cato.org.

Claims and Bounties Under Existing Whistleblower Programs

The frequently offered concern about the Dodd-Frank whistle-blower provision is that it will prompt many baseless reports that will be costly to accused firms. However, the relatively few instances in which would-be whistleblowers—legitimately or not—have made use of the FFCA and ICP suggest that this concern may be overstated.

The Department of Justice recently reported that, for the fiscal year ended September 30, 2010, recoveries under the FFCA totaled roughly $3.0 billion, of which $2.5 billion related to health care fraud recoveries (exclusive of criminal penalties and recoveries passed along to states). Some $2.3 billion of those recoveries were the result of information reported by whistleblowers, who received approximately $385 million in bounties. Since 1986, bounties paid to whistleblowers have totaled a little over $2.8 billion.

[The insert] presents data made available by Taxpayers Against Fraud, an organization that actively encourages individuals to report fraud under the FFCA. The table summarizes FFCA settlements and judgments, bounty payments, and number of new matters reported by whistleblowers (i.e., qui tam matters) during the period from fiscal year 2001 to 2010.

Although there was an increase in the number of whistleblower reports in 2010 (. . . 573, compared to an annual average during the 10-year period of 393), the number of new reports did not change significantly if one were to compare the more recent five-year period to the previous five-year period. Civil settlements over the 10-year period averaged $1.9 billion per year and bounties averaged $226.9 million per year. Average annual settlements and judgments have increased moderately comparing the latest five-year period (mean = $2.4 billion) to the previous five-year period (mean = $ 1.5 billion), while average annual bounties comparing the same periods have not changed significantly (mean of $253 million vs. mean of $201 million).

Taxpayers Against Fraud further reports the number of cases associated with settlements and judgments during the period 2004–2010 ranged from 74 to 145, and the average bounty was $1.6 million per settled case. Settlements and judgments in 2010 were associated with 145 cases, or an average bounty of approximately $2.6 million per settled case. Based on these recent data, approximately 23 percent of whistleblower reports result in a bounty.

The types of matters reported by whistleblowers vary dramatically, but in the current decade many reports have pertained to the over-billing of Medicare and Medicaid. For example, drug maker Schwarz Pharma was found to have sold drugs to Medicaid that had never been approved by the Federal Drug Administration. Recoveries in the case amounted to $22 million and two whistleblowers received a bounty of $1.8 million. In another case, Chicago-area cardiologist Sushil A. Sheth pled guilty in 2010 to billing Medicare (and other entities) over a five-year period for 14,800 procedures that he never performed. In addition to jail time and fines of $24.3 million associated with the criminal case, Sheth also settled the related civil matter for $20 million. The whistleblower was credited with a bounty equal to 17.5 percent of the civil settlement, or $3.5 million.

The IRS's ICP Whistleblower Program

Data on claims under the IRS's ICP are more limited than those of FFCA. [D]ata reported by the IRS to Congress in 2009 [summarizes] collections, bounty payments, and number of bounties paid during the period from fiscal year 2003 to 2008. Annual collections during the period averaged $138 million and bounties averaged $13 million. The number of bounties associated with collections during the period ranged from 169 to 259, suggesting an average bounty of approximately $60,000 per report. These data do not reflect the effect of amendments to the ICP in 2006 removing discretion associated with bounty payments and instituting minimum thresholds for bounty payments.

The IRS reported to Congress that eligible ICP reports in 2008 totaled 1,246 and pertained to 476 taxpayers. Of those reports, 292 represented possible recoveries in excess of $10 million. Also in 2008, 198 investigations were settled, but only eight of those cases met the $2 million underpayment eligibility threshold enacted in 2006 and applicable beginning in fiscal 2009. The IRS also reported its whistleblower office recently increased in size from four to 14 full-time staff, likely in response to increased whistleblower reports and the results of a 2009 audit by the Treasury Department's inspector general for tax administration that reported inadequate processes and procedures for timely pursuit of whistleblower claims.

A recent matter illustrates the complexity of ICP whistleblower reports. In 2007, a former employee of Switzerland-based UBS asserted the bank was guilty of helping American offshore taxpayers avoid U.S. taxes and filed a claim for an ICP whistleblower bounty. The matter resulted in collection of a $780 million settlement and UBS is required to turn over the names of the depositors it assisted. While the whistleblower and his attorney believe he is entitled to an ICP bounty that could ultimately be in the hundreds of millions of dollars, the IRS contends that it should not have to pay any bounty because, during the course of the investigation, the whistleblower pled guilty to a related criminal charge brought by the Department of Justice and is now serving jail time. While employed by UBS, the whistleblower reportedly had an apartment in Geneva and a million-dollar home in Zermatt, Switzerland. It is not clear whether this example is best classified as "no good deed goes unpunished" or as "you can't have your cake and eat it too."

No Cause for Worry

Collectively, these data suggest that although rewards under existing whistleblower programs may be substantial, general use of the programs is not high. New whistleblower reports to either the Department of Justice under the FFCA or the IRS under the ICP totaled 1,625 in 2008. The number of new whistleblower reports under the FFCA has not varied significantly between the most recent five-year period and the preceding five-year period. Although comparable data are not available for the ICP, based on the number of bounties paid under the program there is no reason to believe the number of new reports is increasing—particularly in light of recent changes concerning minimum collection thresholds. In 2008, a total of $225 million in bounties associated with 631 whistleblower reports were paid under the FFCA and ICP.

Similarities between the FFCA, ICP, and Dodd-Frank lead us to believe the use and success of Dodd-Frank may be similar. Neither the FFCA nor the ICP is advertised broadly to individuals who are likely to become aware of fraudulent activities, and there is currently no indication that the Dodd-Frank whistleblower program will be broadly advertised. Historically, both the FFCA and ICP have been underfunded. The nation's current budget deficit and the SEC's recent announcement that it will not meet the Dodd-Frank deadline for establishing and staffing a whistleblower office suggest the program will not receive funding necessary for the timely pursuit of large volumes of whistleblower reports.

To reduce the likelihood employees will bypass companies' internal whistleblower programs in favor of potential bounties that may be gained under Dodd-Frank, some have suggested firms consider changing their whistleblower programs so as to encourage internal reporting, perhaps even instituting firm-sponsored bounties. Our analyses suggest such changes are not necessary. Existing whistleblower programs have received limited use in spite of offered bounties and implementing internal bounties may have unintended consequences, including increases in unwarranted reports and additional administrative costs. Instead, firms should devote resources to reinforcing a "tone at the top" that promotes ethical behavior and legal compliance throughout the organization and encourages employees to use internal whistleblower programs to report any suspected wrongdoing.

Periodical and Internet Sources Bibliography

The following articles have been selected to supplement the diverse views presented in this chapter.

| Dylan Blaylock | "Most Coverage of Whistleblower Motivation Positive . . ." *Government Accountability Project*, May 14, 2010. www.whistleblower .org. |

| Eleanor Bloxham | "How To Encourage the Right Kind of Whistleblowers," *CNNMoney*, June 15, 2011. http:// management.fortune.cnn.com. |

| Elizabeth C. | "What Makes Bradley Manning Tick? The Psychology of Whistleblowers," *Crabby Golightly*, June 2010. www.crabbygolightly .com. |

| CBS Sacramento | "Whistleblower in Baseball Steroid Scandal Explains Motives," March 23, 2011. http://sacramento .cbslocal.com. |

| John Commins | "Whistleblowers Say Money Is Not Their Motivation," *HealthLeaders Media*, May 17, 2010. www .healthleadersmedia.com. |

| Katherine Hobson | "It's Time to Cap Whistleblower Payments, Former Prosecutor Says," *Health Blog—Wall Street Journal*, February 3, 2011. http:// blogs.wsj.com. |

| Elizabeth Judd | "The SEC's Whistleblower Bounty," *Corporate Secretary*, October 28, 2010. www.corporatesecretary .com. |

| Derek Lowe | "Whistleblowers: Paid Too Much?," *In the Pipeline—Corante*, February 8, 2011. http://pipeline.corante .com. |

CHAPTER 2

Do Whistleblowers Compromise National Security?

Chapter Preface

One of the most controversial whistleblowers in history is Mordechai Vanunu. Vanunu was an Israeli nuclear technician who was an opponent of nuclear weapons. In 1986 he revealed details of Israel's top-secret nuclear weapons program to the British press, reporting that Israel had more nuclear weapons than had previously been thought. He was tried and convicted of treason and served eighteen years in prison.

Many critics of Vanunu have argued that his actions threatened Israel's security. Such writers claim that Israel is surrounded by enemies and that the secrecy of its nuclear program was vital to preserving its advantage over, and to deterring, its aggressive neighbors. Italian journalist Giulio Meotti, for example, wrote in a December 1, 2011, article in *Ynetnews* that Vanunu "endangered the security of Israel at a time when Saddam Hussein's Iraq, Iran's ayatollahs [religious leaders], and Syria's [Hafez al-] Assad were making every effort to develop weapons of mass destruction."

Upon Vanunu's release from prison in 2004, Israeli Attorney General Menachem Mazuz said that he still posed "a significant danger to state security," according to Gideon Alon in a March 10, 2004, article in *Haaretz*. Mazuz was worried that Vanunu might reveal further state secrets to the press. Because of such concerns, Vanunu is still not allowed to speak to the foreign press, and he is not allowed to leave Israel. He has been jailed several times since 2004 for speaking to reporters.

Others have argued that, far from endangering Israel, Vanunu's whistleblowing was a courageous stance for peace. Daniel Ellsberg, a famous whistleblower who revealed details of US actions in Vietnam, called Vanunu "my friend, my hero, my brother." He argued in an April 21, 2004, piece in the *Los Angeles Times* that the secrecy around Israel's nuclear weapons program stoked the paranoia of Israel's neighbors and thus encouraged proliferation. According to Ellsberg, it was Israel's secrecy that endangered its own people, and Vanunu's revelations actually served to advance the cause of peace and protect Israel.

Vanunu himself stated, "I have sacrificed my freedom and risked my life in order to expose the danger of nuclear weapons which threatens this whole region. I acted on behalf of all citizens and all of humanity."

The following chapter looks at varying perspectives on the relationship between whistleblowing and national security.

> *"With the injury to our security spanning the immediate to the long-term, the case for the relentless prosecution of leakers within government is irrefutable."*

Those Who Expose National Secrets Should Be Punished

Gabriel Schoenfeld

Gabriel Schoenfeld is a senior fellow at the Hudson Institute and a former senior editor at Commentary. *In the following viewpoint, he argues that national security laws are necessary to protect the American people. He argues that the press should be prosecuted if it publishes information that could endanger Americans. Schoenfeld says that journalists should respect national security laws out of patriotism. However he argues that they have not done so because of their political agendas and out of contempt for the law.*

As you read, consider the following questions:

1. What does Schoenfeld say his real hope was in calling for Bill Keller and others to be prosecuted for revealing state secrets?

2. Why does Schoenfeld believe that leaks stifle collaboration with our allies?

3. According to Schoenfeld, what is one example of a time that the *New York Times* withheld information about a story to protect life?

The Constitution is not a suicide pact, said Justice Robert H. Jackson famously. But how should we contend with those who, for reasons not entirely intellectual, treat one provision of the Constitution as if it were, and would follow their absolutist conception of the First Amendment to the death—or, rather, to the deaths of others? From our nation's inception to the present day our legal system has contained the tools to protect the public from those who would do it harm. Laws enabling prosecution of malefactors—fully constitutional laws—are on the books. Yet they are not being enforced.

Chilling the Press

In the midst of the war on terror the supposedly ultrasecretive [George W.] Bush administration declined to act against the *New York Times* in the face of successive provocations. Barring another murderous strike on our homeland, it is a safe wager that no future administration will act either. Perfectly understandable reasons (to which I have already adverted), fear of both graymail and great political upheaval, underpin the government's reticence. When in the pages of *Commentary* in 2006 I had called for the Justice Department to prosecute the *New York Times* [for revealing details of the Bush Administration's domestic wiretapping program] under the Comint Act, I never for a moment expected it would happen. As I told one interviewer at the time, "Before my essay came out, I would say the chance was zero percent. After the article came out, the odds have risen to .05 percent." Instead of tossing [*Times* editor] Bill Keller and others in jail, my real hope, I explained, was to have set in motion a "chilling effect" on a press that was placing us all at risk.

There is scant evidence that a chill of any sort has descended, although it is striking how thin-skinned some news organizations, the *Times* in particular, have become in their self-presentation when dealing with secrets. The mere fact that Bill Keller has felt it necessary to publish extraordinary statements defending the paper's decision making in [publishing sensitive information] cases reveals a sense within its editorial offices that public tolerance of its behavior is at risk. But at the same time, there is still no reason to doubt that should the right occasion arise—if not this year then next, if not during this administration then during the next—precious secrets of the kind that do genuine damage to our national security will be once again spilled across the front pages of the *Times* and other newspapers. The question I raised in *Commentary*—under what circumstances can and should journalists be prosecuted for publishing government secrets?— remains in want of an answer.

The case for prosecution rests upon the enormous damage such leaks can inflict. Yet the confusion-inducing paradox here is that unless we are particularly unlucky, demonstrating the damage we have suffered or will suffer from a leak in any particular instance will always be an exercise in indeterminacy. We are contending, after all, not only with our own secrets but with those of our adversaries, who themselves engage in concealment and are never so kind as to tell us how they are countering the policies and capabilities divulged by our press. Our government's inability to describe the damage is thus built in to the problem itself and is then twisted around by the media into an additional rationale for behaving heedlessly. No harm, no foul, are the watchwords they repeat.

Yet we live now in a world in which small groups of remorseless men are plotting to strike our buildings, bridges, tunnels, and subways, and seeking to acquire weapons of mass destruction that they would not hesitate to use against our cities, taking the lives of hundreds of thousands or more. To contend with that grim reality, our national-security apparatus inexorably generates more secrets, and more sensitive secrets, and seemingly exercises weaker control over those same vital secrets than ever before. Since time immemorial it has been a basic precept of warfare that disclosure of plans and capabilities to an adversary comes at one's peril. But leaks also stifle collaboration with our allies—an essential component of counterterrorism—who are loath to share their intelligence with us lest their hard-won secrets become public, costing them precious resources and even lives. . . . Not long before September 11 [2001] President [Bill] Clinton, not particularly hawkish in national security matters, echoed the same warning, declaring that leaks "damage our intelligence relationships abroad." They also, he added, "compromise intelligence gathering, jeopardize lives, and increase the threat of terrorism."

The Danger of Leaks

Those are costs of great magnitude, but one must additionally weigh in the balance other less dramatic but no less important exactions imposed by leaks. We have already noted the injury to democratic rule when unelected individuals act to override the public's will. With it also comes the destruction of our government's ability to deliberate in an orderly and coherent fashion. In a system in which a single individual burrowed deep inside a bureaucracy can derail entire policies simply by placing a call to a James Risen or a Seymour Hersh [both journalists], there is constant anxiety that sensitive information will hemorrhage. The consequence is that the most critical decisions taken by the U.S. government must be decided upon by small groups of trusted individuals at the very apex of power. As these decisionmakers guide the ship of state, they are deprived of the enormous pool of expertise available below deck. This is a recipe for dysfunction and paralysis, ensuring that decisions of profound consequence are taken without adequate counsel while some options are altogether foreclosed. The results for our statecraft have all too often spoken for themselves.

With the injury to our security spanning the immediate to the long-term, the case for the relentless prosecution of leakers within government is irrefutable. Yet apprehending leakers has in almost every instance proved fruitless. Given the obstacles in the way of that approach, the case for prosecuting the journalists who operate out in the open would seem to be equally or even more compelling.

Transparency vs. Secrecy

Yet there is another side to the story that must not be brushed aside. Legal action against the press would have undeniable costs to our democracy and our freedom. We cannot lose sight of [the fact] that . . . our national security system is saddled with pervasive mis- and overclassification that remains entrenched despite universal recognition of its existence and numerous attempts at reform. We face the ineradicable potential for misuse of secrecy to obscure incompetence and to promote illicit ends. Closed doors are incubators for corruption and can enable units of government, as in Watergate[1] and the Iran-Contra affair,[2] to depart from the confines of law. Judge [Murray] Gurfein's words in the Pentagon Papers[3] case—that a "ubiquitous press must be suffered by those in authority in order to preserve the even greater values of freedom of expression and the right of the people to know"— are potent and must be acknowledged as such.

The public interest in transparency is diametrically opposed to the public interest in secrecy. With the two desiderata [something desired as a necessity] set in extreme tension, would it truly make sense for the Justice Department to prosecute the press on each and every occasion when it drops classified information into the public domain? Even to an advocate of more stringent security like myself, such an approach would be absurd, a cure that would drain the lifeblood from democratic discourse and kill the patient.

Fortunately there are far more attractive avenues for finding the proper balance. The Pentagon Papers case is once again a lodestar. The road out of our perplexing dilemma was mapped there in a concurring opinion of uncommon eloquence by Justice Potter Stewart, a devoted friend of the press and protector of the First Amendment.

The Constitution entrusts the executive, Stewart wrote, with "largely unshared power" in the realm of foreign policy and national security. The executive thus also bears "the largely unshared duty to determine and preserve the degree of internal security necessary to exercise that power successfully." Being unshared, "it is an awesome responsibility, requiring judgment and wisdom of a high order." A host of considerations "dictate that a very first principle of that wisdom would be an insistence upon avoiding secrecy for its own sake. For when everything is classified, then nothing is classified, and the system becomes one to be disregarded by the cynical or the careless, and to be manipulated by those intent on self-protection or self-promotion."

In the face of the danger of degeneration into a dense web of self-interested secrecy of the sort Stewart is describing, it becomes impossible to quarrel with him that, in the final analysis, "the only effective restraint upon executive policy and power in the areas of national defense and international affairs may lie in an enlightened citizenry—in an informed and critical public opinion which alone can here protect the values of democratic government." For this reason Stewart concluded that "a press that is alert, aware, and free most vitally serves the basic purpose of the First Amendment. For without an informed and free press there cannot be an enlightened people."

But Stewart was thus placing government secrets between a hammer and an anvil. For even as he saw a central role for an informed and free press, he did not blink from asserting the government's overriding right to control information. He concurred with Justice White's holding that the *Times* could well be

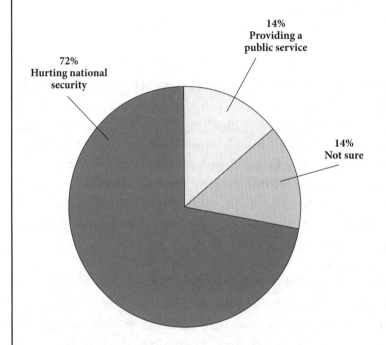

Public Opinion of Media Discretion and National Security

When media outlets release secret government documents, are they hurting national security or providing a public service?

72%
Hurting national security

14%
Providing a public service

14%
Not sure

Results are based on a November 2010 telephone survey of likely US voters.

TAKEN FROM: *Rasmussen Reports*, "51% Say Leaking of U.S. Secrets Is Treason," December 2, 2010. www.rasmussenreports.com/public_content/politics/general_politics/november_2010/51_say_leaking_of_u_s_secrets_is_treason.

criminally liable for publishing secrets. In his own opinion, he stated flatly that "in the area of basic national defense the frequent need for *absolute* secrecy is, of course, self-evident," and "that it is the constitutional duty of the Executive—as a matter of sovereign prerogative . . . to protect the confidentiality necessary to carry out its responsibilities in the fields of international relations and national defense."

The contradiction here is conspicuous. On the one hand Stewart is saying the press must be empowered to keep the American people informed. On the other hand the government must be empowered—indeed it has a "constitutional duty"—to control information. Can this circle be squared?

Government Discretion

It can be. The press, one can readily extrapolate from Stewart's opinion, does and should have an essential checking role on the government in the realm of foreign affairs, national defense, and intelligence. That checking role, if it is to be more than a charade, must extend, as it now does, into the inner workings of the U.S. national security apparatus where secrecy is the coin of the realm. But even as the press strives to carry out this function, this does not mean it should be exempt from the strictures of law. What it *does* mean is that in enforcing the law, the executive must exercise "judgment and wisdom of a high order" and seek to punish the publication only of those secrets that truly endanger national security while giving a pass to all lesser infringements. "The hallmark of a truly effective internal security system," wrote Stewart, "would be the maximum possible disclosure, recognizing that secrecy can best be preserved only when credibility is truly maintained." Prosecutorial discretion is a means to bring about that maximum possible disclosure while seeing to it that genuinely important secrets remain secure.

It is right and proper that jaywalkers are not ticketed for crossing little-trafficked roads. It is also right and proper that they are arrested for wandering onto interstate highways. In this respect the Espionage Act, derided by some as incomprehensible, is drawn with precision. The information it safeguards . . . is not merely secret—the equivalent of casual jaywalking—it must be "National Defense Information," information that is both closely held *and* harmful to the nation if disclosed.

If prosecutors must exercise discretion in their choice of when to prosecute, so too must editors exercise discretion in their choice of what to publish. If they publish secrets whose disclosure is arguably harmless—say, for example, the still-classified CIA budget for fiscal year 1964—or secrets that conceal abuses, say, for example, the cynical manipulation of information "by those intent on self-protection or self-promotion," they should trust that, if indicted by a wayward government, a jury of twelve citizens would evaluate the government's ill-conceived prosecution and vote to acquit. On the other hand, if editors disclose a secret vital to our national security—and have no justification for doing so beyond a desire to regale readers with an "interesting yarn" replete with "startling and amusing tidbits" and haul in a Pulitzer Prize along the way—they should also be prepared to face the judgment of a jury of twelve citizens and, if convicted, the full wrath of the law.

Newspaper editors are fully capable of exercising discretion about sensitive matters when they so choose. A dramatic example came to light in 2009 when the *Times* revealed that it had succeeded for a period of six months in suppressing news that one of its reporters, David Rohde, had been kidnapped in Afghanistan by the Taliban. The editors seemed to exercise the art of concealment with greater success than the U.S. government's own secrecy apparatus is often capable of achieving. Neither the *Times* nor its industry competitors, who readily agreed to gag themselves at the *Times*'s request, published a word about the missing journalist until Rohde escaped his captors and made his way to safety. "We hate sitting on a story," explained Bill Keller. "But sometimes we do. I mean, sometimes we do it because the military or another government agency convinces us that, if we publish information, it will put lives at risk."

All honor to Bill Keller for that. But when the lives of *non-journalists* are on the line, such discretion cannot be—and under our current laws is not—a strictly voluntary affair. Despite Keller's claims the *Times* and other leading newspapers have been far from responsible in their handling of secrets. But even if they were models of rectitude, the public would still be left without recourse in the face of other lesser publications that are not such models, or openly disloyal outlets that might in the future come along, publishing the modern-day equivalent of the sailing dates of transports or the movement of troops. . . .

Unpatriotic Journalists

Back in 1931, in *Near v. Minnesota*, the Supreme Court took it as a given that "*no one would question* but that a government might prevent . . . the publication of the sailing dates of transports or the number and location of troops [emphasis added]." But today journalists almost certainly *would* question. In 1987 two of our country's most famous newsmen, Peter Jennings of ABC and Mike Wallace of CBS, were asked on a television program if they would warn American troops of an impending ambush. The exact question put to them was: Does a journalist "have some higher duty, either patriotic or human, to do something other than just roll film as soldiers from his own country were being shot?" Wallace's immediate response, echoed by a vacillating Jennings, was: "No. You don't have a higher duty. No. No. You're a reporter!"

This appalling stance and the guileless lack of shame with which it was pronounced is precisely the same stance that underpins the publication of national-defense secrets today. The Fourth Estate has changed beyond recognition since the era when [President Franklin] Roosevelt could speak of the "patriotic press," a description that if employed today the press would itself instantly reject. Long gone is the era when a president could come before the press gallery and declare, as John F. Kennedy did in 1961, that "[i]n time of 'clear and present danger,' the courts have held that even the privileged rights of the First Amendment must yield to the public's need for national security" and at the present moment "the danger has never been more clear and its presence has never been more imminent." For such words, an American leader would be greeted with scoffs dipped in acid.

Indeed, with a press now wantonly compromising operational counterterrorism programs, things have swung to an extreme without precedent in our history.

Bill Keller and Dean Baquet [an editor at the *New York Times*] and journalists like them are claiming unfettered freedom of action with accountability to no one but themselves. They refuse to recognize that the law, even a law seldom or never employed as a coercive instrument, is an expression of the public's will. What they fail to see or will not acknowledge is that the statutes protecting national security secrets are not just a mechanical system of sanctions, but, like all laws in a democracy, a moral guidepost, a code by which the press can be judged by the public and by which the press can judge and police itself.

That self-judging and self-policing is not occurring today. To the contrary, America's premier newspaper [that is, the *Times*] is playing the lead part in a drama written during World War II by the diehard isolationist [former owner and publisher of the *Chicago Tribune*, Robert Rutherford] Colonel McCormick. Like McCormick, as they imperil the public, the editors of the *Times* wrap themselves in the mantle of the First Amendment. Like McCormick, they assert, out of a seemingly invincible ignorance, that in publishing whatever they choose no matter the cost, they are carrying out the mandate of the Founding Fathers. In fact things are the other way around; the conduct of the press today raises the question posed by James Schlesinger of whether the free society built by the Founders can defend itself, and not only from external dangers but also from those who would subvert democracy by placing themselves above the law.

Notes

1. Watergate was a scandal during the 1970s in which the Richard Nixon administration was found to be illegally wiretapping political opponents.
2. Iran-Contra was a scandal during the 1980s in which the Ronald Reagan administration was found to be illegally selling arms to Iran to fund rebels in Nicaragua.
3. The Pentagon Papers were US Department of Defense documents about the Vietnam War that were leaked to the *New York Times* in 1971.

> *"Secrecy is a cornerstone of autocratic rule and unaccountable political systems, not democracies."*

Whistleblowers Expose Illegal Activity, Not Government Secrets

Jesselyn Radack

Jesselyn Radack is the homeland security director at the Government Accountability Project and a whistleblower who revealed that the FBI committed an ethics violation in its interrogation of a terror suspect. In the following viewpoint, she argues that national secrecy is often used to cover up crimes or wrongdoing. She says that exposing those crimes through leaks or publication is a public service and protected by the First Amendment. She concludes that crimes, not the exposure of crimes, should be punished.

As you read, consider the following questions:

1. How does Radack say Shoenfeld uses reverse psychology?
2. According to Radack, to whom does the Whistleblower Protection Act allow whistleblowers to make disclosures?

3. Who was the Espionage Act meant to prosecute, according to General Thomas Clark?

G abriel Schoenfeld's book *Necessary Secrets* is very readable and argumentatively seductive. I agree with Schoenfeld [a political scientist] that we should have a meaningful debate about the tension between transparency and secrecy and the appropriate role of the press, especially during national security crises. I also agree with his observation that "war is one of the great engines of secrecy" (though I would also add, one of the great catalysts of government overreaching and infringement of civil liberties.) However, while Schoenfeld identifies a problem—the publication of true facts that are secret—he never plumbs the deeper and more salient question: What if the true and secret facts are illegal?

Security and Secrecy

His central complaint is articulated in the second paragraph of the book: "I was incensed by the publication in the *New York Times* of a series of stories in 2005 and 2006 compromising some of the secret counter-terrorism programs that the U.S. government had initiated." In particular, Schoenfeld takes aim at the explosive Dec. 16, 2005, *Times* article that revealed that President George W. Bush's National Security Agency (NSA) had been spying on American citizens without warrants. Schoenfeld views this as a program the U.S. government had initiated to avert the repetition of another Sept. 11, 2001, but fails to mention that this program became one of the biggest scandals of the Bush administration, which many viewed as its single most flagrant act of lawbreaking.

His solution is that newspaper sources and reporters should face prosecution, be fined or even be sentenced to jail under the Espionage Act of 1917, and he outlines what a "hypothetical prosecution" of the *New York Times* for its revelation of electronic eavesdropping would look like.

Part of the problem with Schoenfeld's argument is that he talks about "national security," but he really means "governmental secrecy." What is done as part of the latter is often justified by the former, but does not necessarily further it, and sometimes is even at odds with it. To buy Schoenfeld's arguments about "the appropriate role of the press in wartime," you must subscribe to his operating premise that "[e]ver since September 11 the country has been at war," a notion in vogue some eight years ago, but one that has been roundly criticized by both liberal and conservative scholars for being an undeclared war of indefinite length. You must also believe that secrecy is just as "an essential prerequisite of self-governance" as openness, a proposition antithetical to the First Amendment, which, properly conceived, is predominantly about the public debate by which America governs itself. Secrecy is a cornerstone of autocratic rule and unaccountable political systems, not democracies.

So, why are Schoenfeld's arguments so palatable? In masterful sophistry, Schoenfeld uses reverse psychology: The *New York Times* failed to "exercise responsibility" and "broke the public trust" by exposing electronic eavesdropping, not the Bush administration or NSA by engaging in it. Whistleblowers like Thomas Tamm violated their oath of secrecy by disclosing the scandal, not the government by violating its oath to uphold the Constitution. Although he characterizes the Watergate[1] and the Iran-Contra[2] affairs as "renegade governmental activity," secret surveillance (a close cousin to the illegality that underpinned Watergate) gets a pass because in some über-paternalistic way it is meant to protect us—and anyone who tries to bring forth information that would allow the public to exercise its sovereign prerogative of democratic debate be damned, or better yet, sent to prison. Isn't incarceration the ultimate way to stifle public debate by cutting off alternative information at the source?

Debunked Arguments

In support of Schoenfeld's novel prosecutorial theory, he trots out many of the old arguments that have been debunked. For example, he states that the Foreign Intelligence Surveillance Act

(FISA) was too "cumbersome." He also dredges up the tired excuse that "advances in telecommunications technology during the two and half decades since FISA was enacted render[ed] it unsuitable" and "[r]equiring a court order to intercept [e-mail] communications was a preposterous barrier to U.S. intelligence gathering." All of this is belied by the fact that FISA was massively expanded in October 2001, at the Bush administration's request, to (in the president's own words) "allow surveillance of all communications used by terrorists, including e-mails, the Internet, and cell phones." After assuring the country that he had all the surveillance tools he needed, Bush proceeded the same month with his secret spying regime.

Schoenfeld acknowledges that Congress could "have adjusted FISA to better suit the NSA's proposed new role," but that for "doctrinal" reasons—which he studiously avoids referring to as the much denounced "unitary executive theory" (that the president has constitutionally unlimited power in wartime)—"[t]he White House opted to circumvent the statute." Yet he assures us, contrary to this assertion and to history, that "[t]he judiciary and the executive branch were collaborating in the midst of a crisis to make a classified program succeed within the confines of law. So too was Congress kept in the loop."

Especially stunning in light of the [Barack] Obama Justice Department's recent grand jury subpoena of one of the reporters who broke the warrantless wiretapping story and its indictment of a former senior NSA official, Thomas Drake, for allegedly disclosing NSA waste and abuse to the press in contravention of various secrecy agreements, Schoenfeld has just a single paragraph in his entire book on whistleblowers, whom he derisively labels as "leakers."

He starts off by stating unequivocally that "officials who uncover illegal conduct in the government are by no means bound by their signature to keep silent and permit violations of law to continue." If that were true, it would negate the entire premise of his book—that *New York Times* sources, reporters and, ideally, the paper itself, should be prosecuted. It would also demand the immediate dismissal of the indictment against Drake. That's because all three federal judges to consider the question have concluded that Bush's NSA program violated criminal law (something Schoenfeld neglects to mention). The clear criminality of the NSA program is further amplified by Schoenfeld's glaring omission of the FISA Amendments Act of 2008—referenced not once in his entire book—which immunized telecommunications companies, terminated all pending lawsuits against them and legalized warrantless wiretapping. It raises the question of why such legislation was necessary, especially the retroactive telecom-immunity provisions, if no law had been broken.

In the next sentence, Schoenfeld states authoritatively that "Congress has enacted 'whistle-blower protection acts' that offer clear and workable procedures for civil servants to report misdeeds and ensure that their complaints will be duly and properly considered." Here's where Schoenfeld is really out of his depth. First of all, the primary whistleblower law, the Whistleblower Protection Act of 1989, does not even cover FBI and intelligence agency whistleblowers. Second, it is riddled with problems. Since 2000, only three out of 53 whistleblowers have received final rulings in their favor from the Merit Systems Protection Board. The U.S. Court of Appeals for the Federal Circuit, which has monopoly jurisdiction over federal whistleblower appeals of administrative decisions, has consistently ruled against them, with whistleblowers winning only three cases out of 205 since October 1994, when Congress last strengthened the law.

Misstating Whistleblower Protections

Schoenfeld states, incorrectly, that "[w]hen classified matters are at issue, these procedures include direct appeals to the Justice Department and to members of the intelligence committees in Congress." This could have been clarified if Schoenfeld bothered to read the two-page Intelligence Community Whistleblower

Protection Act of 1998. Before going to congressional intelligence committees, an employee must get preclearance from the agency inspector general. It gets worse. Although not a model of legislative drafting, this law requires the employee to go through the agency inspector general even if that inspector general does not find the employee's complaint credible. This kangaroo process is a transparent attempt to keep employees from going to Congress in violation of the First Amendment, the Lloyd-La Folette Act and various anti-gag statutes. Not surprisingly, only three such complaints have been made to the Defense Department since 1998.

Finally, Schoenfeld states, also incorrectly, that whistleblower procedures "emphatically do not include . . . disclosing to . . . the *New York Times.*" The Whistleblower Protection Act specifically permits a government employee to make disclosures of any information that the employee reasonably believes evidences a violation of any law, rule or regulation; gross mismanagement or waste of funds; abuse of authority; or a substantial and specific danger to public health or safety. It permits disclosure to be made not only to another official of the executive branch but to anyone—a reporter, a member of Congress or an interest-group representative. This has been well-supported by legislative history and case law from the Federal Circuit, which is hardly a friend of whistleblowers. The media are independent entities, such as Congress, to which disclosures may be made. In fact, courts have held, counterintuitively, that complaints to a supervisor about the supervisor's own conduct are not disclosures covered by the Whistleblower Protection Act, but disclosures to the press are protected.

To the extent that Schoenfeld is apoplectic about *New York Times* revelations, one can only imagine what he thinks of WikiLeaks [an international non-profit dedicated to publishing leaked documents]. I submit, however, that the answer lies in meaningful whistleblower protections, not retaliatory criminal prosecutions.

Retrospective Symmetry

Schoenfeld decries "retrospective symmetry," in which a vision of the past is imposed upon the present. He almost sounds like a liberal when he says: "It will not do to . . . hold up the handiwork of the Founding Fathers as a template for our contemporary circumstances. . . . We enter this historical terrain not out of some originalist impulse to embrace the standards of the eighteenth century and impose them on our own institutions." Yet he does not hesitate to graft modern words like "leaking" and "terrorism" onto his revisionist interpretation of history.

Perhaps Schoenfeld should move to England, where they have an Official Secrets Act, which punishes both the source and the publisher of secret government materials. Instead, Schoenfeld advocates bypassing Congress (anyone detect a trend here?) to create what is tantamount to a state secrets act by urging prosecution under the Espionage Act, thus doing an end-run around the democratic legislative process he insists he believes in. In a key chapter, Schoenfeld outlines a "hypothetical prosecution" of the *New York Times*. Although Schoenfeld takes credit for this idea, a number of scholars and judges have for years argued about the applicability of the Espionage Act's sweeping § 793 provision to the press. I will leave to others more expert in the area the arguments about why the First Amendment should immunize reporters conducting good-faith investigations for stories of public concern, even if they could technically be held liable under a broad inchoate theory of liability under the Espionage Act.

What is more disturbing is Schoenfeld's application of §793(e)'s vast language to whistleblowers. In the 93 years of its existence, there have been only three prosecutions of "leakers" under the Espionage Act, which would seemingly counsel hesitation in using it to prosecute them as spies: the unsuccessful prosecution of Daniel Ellsberg and Anthony Russo in 1971 for disclosing the Pentagon Papers [Defense Department documents about Vietnam]; the 1985 conviction of Samuel Morison—later pardoned by President Bill Clinton—for leaking U.S. satellite

© 2008 by Adam Zyglis and Cagle Cartoons.com.

photos to a military-related magazine focusing on defense planning, weapons technology and world security threats; and the aborted 2005 indictment of two employees of the American-Israel Public Affairs Committee on charges of unauthorized receipt and transmittal of classified information—the first time the Espionage Act has been used against private citizens for doing nothing more than what other lobbyists and journalists do all the time. None of these men were spies. None betrayed the United States or intended to harm it. They neither gave nor sold information to foreign governments.

Moreover, Congress never intended for the statute to have such broad effect. From its inception, the Espionage Act engendered fears about its seemingly wide-ranging applicability. Sens. Lee Overman (D-N.C.) and Key Pittman (D-Nev.) emphasized during the 1917 debates that "[t]he object of the act is to punish a man guilty of a crime, and that crime consists of spying on this Government." Sen. Pat McCarran (D-Nev.) (hardly a champion of civil liberties, he is best known for the McCarran-Walter Act, a bill that empowered the government to deny visas for ideological reasons) asked Attorney General Thomas Clark to allay similar fears in the 1949 debate over amending the Espionage Act, which occurred the next year. Clark assured him, "Nobody other than a spy, saboteur, or other person who would weaken the internal security of the Nation need have any fear of prosecution under either existing law or the provisions of this bill." Later, as a U.S. Supreme Court justice, Clark voted to strike down as unconstitutional President [Harry] Truman's seizure of the nation's steel mills to end a strike in *Youngstown Sheet & Tube Co. v. Sawyer*, 343 U.S. 579 (1952)—the landmark case on presidential power in wartime, which limited the power of the president to act without explicit constitutional authority or congressional approval, that the Justice Department memos justifying secret surveillance neglected to cite.

Punish the Crime, Not the Exposure

Overly broad, ambiguous laws have an irresistible quality, and now—ignoring the president's own edict to "look forward, not backward"—the Obama administration, through its marching orders to Attorney General Eric Holder Jr., has literally taken a page from Schoenfeld's book by forcing a trial for espionage on a person who is not a spy: Thomas Drake. Unfortunately, the Espionage Act does not distinguish between spying and "leaking." A hurdle in the Drake prosecution will be demonstrating to a jury that he had the requisite state of mind that is a crucial element of the crime. Specifically, did he have "reason to believe" that his disclosure—if he made one at all—"could be used to the injury of the United States"? There is more than a reasonable doubt that Drake had any such state of mind. When Drake went to a reporter, it was only after his internal complaints fell on the deaf ears of his bosses, the NSA's general counsel and inspector general, the Defense Department's inspector general and the House and Senate intelligence committees. His disclosures were a matter of public concern and were clearly of public significance: The NSA went on a "billion dollar boondoggle" and ultimately chose an extremely intrusive surveillance program over an even better program that protected privacy.

In a logical absurdity, if you subscribe to Schoenfeld's argument, sources who disclose information to reporters would be criminally liable, reporters who then write about it for newspapers would be liable, the newspapers that publish the information would be liable, and by extension, any readers would be liable, especially if they e-mail the article, discuss it or disseminate it any further. The old adage goes, "it's not the crime, but the cover-up" that will ultimately get bad actors. Under this calculus, at least malfeasors are held accountable at some point. But Schoenfeld's version appears to be "it's not the crime—ever—but the exposure of it" that will be penalized. I submit that when secrecy is used to cloak illegal conduct, that is what should be punished.

Notes

1. Watergate was a scandal during the 1970s in which the Richard Nixon administration was found to be illegally wiretapping political opponents.
2. Iran-Contra was a scandal during the 1980s in which the Ronald Reagan administration was found to be illegally selling arms to Iran to fund rebels in Nicaragua.

> *"The FBI takes very seriously allegations involving government employees who willfully retain or disclose classified information they are not authorized to possess."*

Whistleblower Thomas Drake Compromised Classified Information

United States Department of Justice

The United States Department of Justice (DOJ) is the executive US federal government department responsible for law enforcement. In the following viewpoint, the DOJ states that it has prepared an indictment against Thomas Drake, an executive with the National Security Agency (NSA). The indictment states that Drake willfully leaked classified information to a reporter. The indictment says that Drake attempted to cover up his actions, and then lied to FBI officials about having leaked the information. The indictment accuses Drake of willful retention of classified documents and obstruction of justice.

"Former NSA Senior Executive Charged with Illegally Retaining Classified Information, Obstructing Justice and Making False Statements," justice.gov, United States Department of Justice, April 15, 2010.

As you read, consider the following questions:
1. List three steps the indictment alleges that Drake took to facilitate the provision of information to the reporter.
2. What conditions is it alleged that Drake required the reporter to agree to?
3. Why specifically has Drake been charged with obstruction of justice, according to the Department of Justice?

A federal grand jury in the District of Maryland has returned a 10-count indictment charging former National Security Agency (NSA) senior executive Thomas A. Drake with the willful retention of classified information, obstruction of justice and making false statements, announced Assistant Attorney General Lanny A. Breuer of the Criminal Division.

Transmitting Classified Documents

According to the indictment, Drake, 52, was a high-ranking NSA employee from 2001 through 2008, where he had access to highly classified documents and information. The indictment alleges that between approximately February 2006 and November 2007, a newspaper reporter published a series of articles about the NSA. The indictment alleges that Drake served as a source for many of those articles, including articles that contained classified information. The indictment also alleges that Drake took a series of steps to facilitate the provision of this information to the reporter, including:

- exchanging hundreds of e-mails with and meeting with the reporter;
- researching stories for the reporter to write in the future by e-mailing unwitting NSA employees and accessing classified and unclassified documents on classified NSA networks;

- copying and pasting classified and unclassified information from NSA documents into untitled word processing documents which, when printed, had the classification markings removed;
- printing both classified and unclassified documents, bringing them to his home, and retaining them there without authority;
- scanning and e-mailing electronic copies of classified and unclassified documents to the reporter from his home computer; and
- reviewing, commenting on, and editing drafts of the reporter's articles.

"As alleged, this defendant used a secret, non-government e-mail account to transmit classified and unclassified information that he was not authorized to possess or disclose. As if those allegations are not serious enough, he also allegedly later shredded documents and lied about his conduct to federal agents in order to obstruct their investigation," said Assistant Attorney General Lanny A. Breuer. "Our national security demands that the sort of conduct alleged here—violating the government's trust by illegally retaining and disclosing classified information—be prosecuted and prosecuted vigorously."

"The FBI takes very seriously allegations involving government employees who willfully retain or disclose classified information they are not authorized to possess. Working with prosecutors, we will continue to investigate and pursue charges against these individuals whose actions cannot be justified or tolerated," said Arthur M. Cummings II, FBI Executive Assistant Director, National Security Branch.

Obstruction of Justice

The indictment alleges that Drake received training regarding the protection of classified information, including the instruction not to remove classified information from the NSA. The indictment also alleges that Drake signed acknowledgments affirming that any documents or information he intended for public disclosure were required to be submitted to the NSA for pre-publication review. At no time, according to the indictment, did the NSA authorize Drake to de-classify information or to disclose classified information to unauthorized persons, nor did the NSA authorize Drake to copy and print classified information in a manner that removed its classification markings or to possess classified documents or information at his home.

The indictment alleges that in approximately November 2005, a former congressional staffer asked Drake to speak with a reporter. Between November 2005 and February 2006, according to the indictment, Drake signed up for a free account and then paid for a premium account with an e-mail service that enabled its users to exchange secure e-mails without disclosing the sender or recipient's identity. Using an alias, Drake allegedly then contacted the reporter and volunteered to disclose information about the NSA. The indictment alleges that Drake directed the reporter to create the reporter's own secure e-mail account. After the reporter created such an account, Drake also allegedly required the reporter to agree to certain conditions, including never revealing Drake's identity; attributing information gathered from Drake to a "senior intelligence official"; never using Drake as a single source for information; never telling Drake who the reporter's other sources were; and not commenting on what people, to whom Drake recommended the reporter speak, said to the reporter.

Drake allegedly attempted to conceal his relationship with the reporter and prevent the discovery of evidence linking Drake to his retention of classified documents after the FBI began a criminal investigation into the disclosure of classified information. Specifically, Drake allegedly shredded classified and unclassified documents, including his handwritten notes that he had removed from the NSA; deleted classified and unclassified information on his home computer; and made false statements to FBI agents.

The indictment charges Drake with five counts of willfully retaining documents that relate to the national defense. These include four classified e-mails and an additional classified document. In addition, the indictment charges Drake with obstruction of justice for allegedly destroying and deleting documents with the intent to impede and obstruct the federal investigation into alleged disclosures of classified information. The indictment also charges Drake with four counts of making false statements to FBI agents.

Willful retention of classified documents carries a maximum penalty of 10 years in prison. Obstruction of justice carries a maximum penalty of 20 years in prison. The charge of making a false statement carries a maximum penalty of five years in prison. Each of the charged counts carries a maximum fine of $250,000.

The case is being prosecuted by Senior Litigation Counsel William M. Welch II of the Criminal Division and Trial Attorney John P. Pearson of the Criminal Division's Public Integrity Section. This case is being investigated by the FBI and the NSA Office of Security & Counterintelligence. The National Security Division also provided assistance in this matter.

An indictment is merely an allegation. Defendants are presumed innocent unless proven guilty in a court of law.

| "I did not tell secrets. I am facing prison for having raised an alarm, period."

The Prosecution of Whistleblower Thomas Drake Is Unjust

Jane Mayer

Jane Mayer is an investigative journalist and a staff writer for the New Yorker. *In the following viewpoint, she argues that National Security Agency (NSA) executive Thomas Drake did not leak important classified information to the press. Instead, she says, he exposed waste, fraud, and possible illegal activity in the agency. She suggests he is being prosecuted for embarrassing the NSA. She concludes that such prosecutions protect the government from accountability and encourage mismanagement, fraud, and civil rights abuses.*

As you read, consider the following questions:

1. According to Steven Aftergood, what does the government want the Drake case to be about and what does the defense want the case to be about?

2. What major leak occurred in December 2005, according to Mayer?

3. Who is Thomas Tamm, and why does Mayer say he is particularly concerned about the Drake prosecution?

On June 13th [2011], a fifty-four-year-old former government employee named Thomas Drake is scheduled to appear in a courtroom in Baltimore, where he will face some of the gravest charges that can be brought against an American citizen. A former senior executive at the National Security Agency [NSA], the government's electronic-espionage service, he is accused, in essence, of being an enemy of the state. According to a ten-count indictment delivered against him in April, 2010, Drake violated the Espionage Act—the 1917 statute that was used to convict Aldrich Ames, the C.I.A. officer who, in the eighties and nineties, sold U.S. intelligence to the K.G.B. [the national security agency of the Soviet Union], enabling the Kremlin to assassinate informants. In 2007, the indictment says, Drake willfully retained top-secret defense documents that he had sworn an oath to protect, sneaking them out of the intelligence agency's headquarters, at Fort Meade, Maryland, and taking them home, for the purpose of "unauthorized disclosure." The aim of this scheme, the indictment says, was to leak government secrets to an unnamed newspaper reporter, who is identifiable as Siobhan Gorman, of the *Baltimore Sun*. Gorman wrote a prize-winning series of articles for the *Sun* about financial waste, bureaucratic dysfunction, and dubious legal practices in N.S.A. counterterrorism programs. Drake is also charged with obstructing justice and lying to federal law-enforcement agents. If he is convicted on all counts, he could receive a prison term of thirty-five years.

Prosecuting Leaks

The government argues that Drake recklessly endangered the lives of American servicemen. "This is not an issue of benign documents," William M. Welch II, the senior litigation counsel who is prosecuting the case, argued at a hearing in March, 2010. The N.S.A., he went on, collects "intelligence for the soldier in the field. So when individuals go out and they harm that ability, our intelligence goes dark and our soldier in the field gets harmed."

Top officials at the Justice Department describe such leak prosecutions as almost obligatory. Lanny Breuer, the Assistant Attorney General who supervises the department's criminal division, told me, "You don't get to break the law and disclose classified information just because you want to." He added, "Politics should play no role in it whatsoever."

When President Barack Obama took office, in 2009, he championed the cause of government transparency, and spoke admiringly of whistle-blowers, whom he described as "often the best source of information about waste, fraud, and abuse in government." But the Obama Administration has pursued leak prosecutions with a surprising relentlessness. Including the Drake case, it has been using the Espionage Act to press criminal charges in five alleged instances of national-security leaks—more such prosecutions than have occurred in all previous Administrations combined. The Drake case is one of two that Obama's Justice Department has carried over from the [President George W.] Bush years.

Gabriel Schoenfeld, a conservative political scientist at the Hudson Institute, who, in his book *Necessary Secrets* (2010), argues for more stringent protection of classified information, says, "Ironically, Obama has presided over the most draconian crackdown on leaks in our history—even more so than Nixon."

Political Reprisal

One afternoon in January [2011], Drake met with me, giving his first public interview about this case. He is tall, with thinning sandy hair framing a domed forehead, and he has the erect bearing of a member of the Air Force, where he served before joining the N.S.A., in 2001. Obsessive, dramatic, and emotional, he has an unwavering belief in his own rectitude. Sitting at a Formica table at the Tastee Diner, in Bethesda, Drake—who is a registered Republican—groaned and thrust his head into his hands. "I actually had hopes for Obama," he said. He had not only expected the President to roll back the prosecutions launched by the Bush Administration; he had thought that Bush Administration officials would be investigated for overstepping the law in the "war on terror."

"But power is incredibly destructive," Drake said. "It's a weird, pathological thing. I also think the intelligence community coöpted Obama, because he's rather naïve about national security. He's accepted the fear and secrecy. We're in a scary space in this country."

The Justice Department's indictment narrows the frame around Drake's actions, focusing almost exclusively on his handling of what it claims are five classified documents. But Drake sees his story as a larger tale of political reprisal, one that he fears the government will never allow him to air fully in court. "I'm a target," he said. "I've got a bull's-eye on my back." He continued, "I did not tell secrets. I am facing prison for having raised an alarm, period. I went to a reporter with a few key things: fraud, waste, and abuse, and the fact that there were legal alternatives to the Bush Administration's 'dark side'"—in particular, warrantless domestic spying by the N.S.A.

The indictment portrays him not as a hero but as a treacherous man who violated "the government trust." Drake said of the prosecutors, "They can say what they want. But the F.B.I. can find something on anyone."

Steven Aftergood, the director of the Project on Government Secrecy at the Federation of American Scientists, says of the Drake case, "The government wants this to be about unlawfully retained information. The defense, meanwhile, is painting a picture of a public-interested whistle-blower who struggled to bring attention to what he saw as multibillion-dollar mismanagement."

Because Drake is not a spy, Aftergood says, the case will "test whether intelligence officers can be convicted of violating the Espionage Act even if their intent is pure." He believes that the trial may also test whether the nation's expanding secret intelligence bureaucracy is beyond meaningful accountability. "It's a much larger debate than whether a piece of paper was at a certain place at a certain time," he says.

Jack Balkin, a liberal law professor at Yale, agrees that the increase in leak prosecutions is part of a larger transformation. "We are witnessing the bipartisan normalization and legitimization of a national-surveillance state," he says. In his view, zealous leak prosecutions are consonant with other political shifts since 9/11: the emergence of a vast new security bureaucracy, in which at least two and a half million people hold confidential, secret, or top-secret clearances; huge expenditures on electronic monitoring, along with a reinterpretation of the law in order to sanction it; and corporate partnerships with the government that have transformed the counterterrorism industry into a powerful lobbying force. Obama, Balkin says, has "systematically adopted policies consistent with the second term of the Bush Administration."

Transparency vs. Security

On March 28th, Obama held a meeting in the White House with five advocates for greater transparency in government. During the discussion, the President drew a sharp distinction between whistle-blowers who exclusively reveal wrongdoing and those who jeopardize national security. The importance of maintaining secrecy about the impending raid [May 2, 2011] on [terrorist leader] Osama bin Laden's compound was likely on Obama's mind. The White House has been particularly bedeviled by the ongoing release of classified documents by WikiLeaks, the group led by Julian Assange. Last year, WikiLeaks began releasing a vast trove of sensitive government documents allegedly leaked by a U.S. soldier, Bradley Manning; the documents included references to a courier for bin Laden who had moved his family to Abbottabad—the town where bin Laden was hiding out. Manning has been charged with "aiding the enemy."

Danielle Brian, the executive director of the Project on Government Oversight, attended the meeting, and said that Obama's tone was generally supportive of transparency. But when the subject of national-security leaks came up, Brian said, "the President shifted in his seat and leaned forward. He said this may be where we have some differences. He said he doesn't want to protect the people who leak to the media war plans that could impact the troops." Though Brian was impressed with Obama's overall stance on transparency, she felt that he might be misinformed about some of the current leak cases. She warned Obama that prosecuting whistle-blowers would undermine his legacy. Brian had been told by the White House to avoid any "ask"s on specific issues, but she told the President that, according to his own logic, Drake was exactly the kind of whistle-blower who deserved protection. . . .

A Stunning Leak

In December, 2005, the N.S.A.'s culture of secrecy was breached by a stunning leak. The *Times* reporters James Risen and Eric Lichtblau revealed that the N.S.A. was running a warrantless wiretapping program inside the United States. The paper's editors had held onto the scoop for more than a year, weighing the propriety of publishing it. According to Bill Keller, the executive editor of the *Times*, President Bush pleaded with the paper's editors to not publish the story; Keller told *New York* that "the basic message was: You'll have blood on your hands." After the paper defied the Administration, Bush called the leak "a shameful act." At his command, federal agents launched a criminal investigation to identify the paper's source.

The *Times* story shocked the country. Democrats, including then Senator Obama, denounced the program as illegal and demanded congressional hearings. A FISA [Foreign Intelligence

Surveillance Act] court judge resigned in protest. In March, 2006, Mark Klein, a retired A.T. & T. employee, gave a sworn statement to the Electronic Frontier Foundation, which was filing a lawsuit against the company, describing a secret room in San Francisco where powerful Narus computers appeared to be sorting and copying all of the telecom's Internet traffic—both foreign and domestic. A high-capacity fibre-optic cable seemed to be forwarding this data to a centralized location, which, Klein surmised, was N.S.A. headquarters. Soon, *USA Today* reported that A.T. & T., Verizon, and BellSouth had secretly opened their electronic records to the government, in violation of communications laws. Legal experts said that each instance of spying without a warrant was a serious crime, and that there appeared to be hundreds of thousands of infractions.

President Bush and Administration officials assured the American public that the surveillance program was legal, although new legislation was eventually required to bring it more in line with the law. They insisted that the traditional method of getting warrants was too slow for the urgent threats posed by international terrorism. And they implied that the only domestic surveillance taking place involved tapping phone calls in which one speaker was outside the U.S.

Drake says of Bush Administration officials, "They were lying through their teeth. They had chosen to go an illegal route, and it wasn't because they had no other choice." He also believed that the Administration was covering up the full extent of the program. "The phone calls were the tip of the iceberg. The really sensitive stuff was the data mining." He says, "I was faced with a crisis of conscience. What do I do—remain silent, and complicit, or go to the press?"

Drake has a wife and five sons, the youngest of whom has serious health problems, and so he agonized over the decision. He researched the relevant legal statutes and concluded that if he spoke to a reporter about unclassified matters the only risk he ran was losing his job. N.S.A. policy forbids initiating contact with the press. "I get that it's grounds for 'We have to let you go,'" he says. But he decided that he was willing to lose his job. "This was a violation of everything I knew and believed as an American. We were making the [Richard] Nixon Administration [known for its illegal activities] look like pikers."

Drake got in touch with Gorman, who covered the N.S.A. for the *Baltimore Sun*. He had admired an article of hers and knew that [Diane] Roark [a congressional staff member] had spoken to her previously, though not about anything classified. He got Gorman's contact information from Roark, who warned him to be careful. She knew that in the past the N.S.A. had dealt harshly with people who embarrassed it.

Drake set up a secure Hushmail e-mail account and began sending Gorman anonymous tips. Half in jest, he chose the pseudonym The Shadow Knows. He says that he insisted on three ground rules with Gorman: neither he nor she would reveal his identity; he wouldn't be the sole source for any story; he would not supply her with classified information. But a year into the arrangement, in February, 2007, Drake decided to blow his cover, surprising Gorman by showing up at the newspaper and introducing himself as The Shadow Knows. He ended up meeting with Gorman half a dozen times. But, he says, "I never gave her anything classified." Gorman has not been charged with wrongdoing, and declined, through her lawyer, Laura Handman, to comment, citing the pending trial.

Starting on January 29, 2006, Gorman, who now works at the *Wall Street Journal*, published a series of articles about problems at the N.S.A. . . .

Not Highly Classified

At the time, the government did not complain that the *Sun* had crossed a legal line. It did not contact the paper's editors or try to restrain the paper from publishing Gorman's work. A former N.S.A. colleague of Drake's says he believes that the *Sun* stories revealed government secrets. Others disagree. Steven Aftergood, the secrecy expert, says that the articles "did not damage national security."

Matthew Aid argues that the material Drake provided to the *Sun* should not have been highly classified—if it was—and in any case only highlighted that "the N.S.A. was a management nightmare, which wasn't a secret in Washington." In his view, Drake "was just saying, 'We're not doing our job, and it's having a deleterious effect on mission performance.' He was right, by the way." The *Sun* series, Aid says, was "embarrassing to N.S.A. management, but embarrassment to the U.S. government is not a criminal offense in this country." (Aid has a stake in this debate. In 1984, when he was in the Air Force, he spent several months in the stockade for having stored classified documents in a private locker. The experience, he says, sensitized him to issues of government secrecy.)

While the *Sun* was publishing its series, twenty-five federal agents and five prosecutors were struggling to identify the *Times'* source. The team had targeted some two hundred possible suspects, but had found no culprits. The *Sun* series attracted the attention of the investigators, who theorized that its source might also have talked to the *Times*. This turned out not to be true. . . . "It's sad," an intelligence expert says. "I think they were aiming at the *Times* leak and found this instead." . . .

Classified vs. Unclassified

It wasn't until the morning of November 28, 2007, that he [Drake] saw armed agents streaming across his lawn. Though Drake was informed of his right to remain silent, he viewed the raid as a fresh opportunity to blow the whistle. He spent the day at his kitchen table, without a lawyer, talking. . . but found that the investigators weren't interested in the details of a defunct computer system, or in cost overruns, or in the constitutional conflicts posed by warrantless surveillance. Their focus was on the *Times* leak. He assured them that he wasn't the source, but he confirmed his contact with the *Sun*, insisting that he had not

Bush's Warrantless Wiretapping Program

Once the warrantless wiretapping program became public, the [George W. Bush] Administration's denials switched to attempts at justification. In December 2005, after the *New York Times* ran the story that the Administration had engaged in various warrantless wiretapping programs, President Bush admitted to at least portions of the program. Under one description, the NSA [National Security Agency] targeted international communications when there was cause to believe that at least one party to the communication was outside of the United States and was a member or agent of [terrorist organization] al Qaeda or an associated terrorist organization.

The notion that collection was permissible when only one party to the conversation was outside of the United States ("one-end-foreign") directly contradicted the common understanding that collection of communications within the United States was covered by the Fourth Amendment and FISA [the 1978 Foreign Intelligence Surveillance Act]. FISA *specifically* applied to the "interception of international wire communications to or from any person (whether or not a U.S. person) within the United States without the consent of at least one party." And yet, in defending the President' surveillance program, the Administration claimed that such interceptions were legal, and acted as though this had never been in question.

House Committee on the Judiciary
Majority Staff Report to Chairman John
Conyers Jr., Reigning In the Imperial
Presidency, *January 13, 2009, pp. 155–156.*

relayed any classified information. He also disclosed his computer password. The agents bagged documents, computers, and books, and removed eight or ten boxes of office files from his basement. "I felt incredibly violated," he says.

For four months, Drake continued coöperating. He admitted that he had given Gorman information that he had cut and pasted from secret documents, but stressed that he had not included anything classified. He acknowledged sending Gorman hundreds of e-mails. Then, in April 2008, the F.B.I. told him that someone important wanted to meet with him, at a secure building in Calverton, Maryland. Drake agreed to the appointment. Soon after he showed up, he says, Steven Tyrrell, the prosecutor, walked in and told him, "You're screwed, Mr. Drake. We have enough evidence to put you away for most of the rest of your natural life."

Prosecutors informed Drake that they had found classified documents in the boxes in his basement—the indictment cites three—and discovered two more in his e-mail archive. They also accused him of shredding other documents, and of deleting e-mails in the months before he was raided, in an attempt to obstruct justice. Further, they said that he had lied when he told federal agents that he hadn't given Gorman classified information.

"They had made me into an enemy of the state just by saying I was," Drake says. . . . Drake says that if the boxes did, in fact, contain classified documents he didn't realize it. (The indictment emphasizes that he "willfully" retained documents.) The two documents that the government says it extracted from his e-mail archive were even less sensitive, Drake says. . . . "After charging him with having this ostensibly serious classified document, the government waved a wand and decided it wasn't so classified after all," [Jesselyn] Radack [of the Government Accountability Project] says.

Clearly, the intelligence community hopes that the Drake case will send a message about the gravity of exposing government secrets. But Drake's lawyer, a federal public defender named James Wyda, argued in court last spring that "there have never been two documents so benign that are the subject of this kind of prosecution against a client whose motives are as salutary as Tom's."

Drake insists, too, that the only computer files he destroyed were routine trash: "I held then, and I hold now, I had nothing to destroy." Drake, who left the N.S.A. in 2008, and now works at an Apple Store outside Washington, asks, "Why didn't I erase everything on my computer, then? I know how to do it. They found what they found." . . .

Prosecuting Only Whistleblowers

Few people are more disturbed about Drake's prosecution than the others who spoke out against the N.S.A. surveillance program. In 2008, Thomas Tamm, a Justice Department lawyer, revealed that he was one of the people who leaked to the *Times*. He says of Obama, "It's so disappointing from someone who was a constitutional-law professor, and who made all those campaign promises." The Justice Department recently confirmed that it won't pursue charges against Tamm. Speaking before Congress, Attorney General Holder explained that "there is a balancing that has to be done . . . between what our national-security interests are and what might be gained by prosecuting a particular individual." The decision provoked strong criticism from Republicans, underscoring the political pressures that the Justice Department faces when it backs off such prosecutions. Still, Tamm questions why the Drake case is proceeding, given that Drake never revealed anything as sensitive as what appeared in the *Times*. "The program he talked to the Baltimore *Sun* about was a failure and wasted billions of dollars," Tamm says. "It's embarrassing to the N.S.A., but it's not giving aid and comfort to the enemy."

Mark Klein, the former A.T. & T. employee who exposed the telecom-company wiretaps, is also dismayed by the Drake case. "I think it's outrageous," he says. "The Bush people have been let off. The telecom companies got immunity. The only people Obama has prosecuted are the whistle-blowers."

| "We are concerned about individuals just coming onto our places and taking video without the owners knowing."

Whistleblowers Can Endanger National Food Supplies

Annette Sweeney, interviewed by Katerina Lorenzatos Makris

Annette Sweeney is an Iowa state representative; Katerina Lorenzatos Makris is a novelist and journalist whose articles have appeared in National Geographic Traveler, Mother Jones, *and other outlets. In the following viewpoint, Sweeney argues that it is dangerous for strangers to come onto a farm to take video or pictures. She says that people can bring viruses or disease onto farms. Therefore, she says, if there are concerns about health or animal rights issues on farms, people should contact the sheriff. If they go onto a farm to take pictures, she says, they will be prosecuted.*

As you read, consider the following questions:

1. What groups does Makris say have released videos and photos from farms in recent years, and what have these videos and photos resulted in?

2. According to Sweeney, what amendments to her bill came out of the Iowa House?
3. What does Sweeney say a farmworker should do if he or she notices a problem on the farm and wants to take a picture of it to alert authorities?

As part of a series of articles about a proposed law that would restrict undercover video and photography of possible animal abuse on Iowa farms, *Animal Policy Examiner* recently spoke by telephone with Iowa state Rep. Annette Sweeney, chief sponsor of the bill. Please see Q&A [question and answer] below.

Background on the Proposed Law

House File (HF) 589 would make it a felony to obtain unauthorized video and photos on Iowa crop and animal agriculture facilities, and impose penalties of prison time and fines that would be more severe than for the animal abuse such images might seek to expose.

Animal protection groups including Mercy for Animals, Compassion Over Killing, PETA [People for the Ethical Treatment of Animals], and The Humane Society of the United States have released a number of such videos and photos in recent years, with some resulting in law enforcement investigations, prosecutions, convictions, fines, and closures of animal agriculture facilities.

Many observers are concerned that the bill would violate the First Amendment right to free speech, inhibit whistleblowers, and set a precedent for other states to follow. A similar bill is pending in the Florida legislature.

Q&A with Representative Annette Sweeney

Sweeney owns a cattle farm in central Iowa, where she lives along with thirteen chickens, a cat, and a rescued golden retriever.

Animal Policy Examiner: Right now the bill as I understand it cleared the Senate Ag [Agriculture] Committee?

Rep. Annette Sweeney: Yes it did. It cleared the Senate Ag Committee yesterday [March 30, 2011].

So now what happens?

It will go to the Senate floor for debate and hopefully passage. Hopefully that will happen maybe sometime next week [week of April 3]. I'm not sure, but we're hoping.

Were there any amendments to it?

Coming out of the Ag Committee, no amendments at this time. But we did have amendments that took dogs and cats out, coming out of the House side.

I know there were concerns from some legislators that companion animal facilities [such as dog and cat breeders, pet stores, and animal shelters] would be included.

Yeah, so we addressed that and got it straightened out.

Why do you feel that a bill like this is necessary in Iowa?

I look at it as updating code, because right now in code 90 percent of the bill is already in law. And this updates to where we are concerned about individuals just coming onto our places and taking video without the owners knowing—or pictures—and when you come onto somebody's place, you can have a virus or disease on your person. It's amazing. I think that if people realized how much that people carry on their person, it is rather scary.

And so what we're trying to do with this is if somebody sees abuse—it's already in code—you're supposed to go, and there's proper authorities, go to the sheriff, go to a deputy, go to your county supervisor, you go to report it to the Iowa Department of Agriculture and Land Stewardship, or to the USDA [United States Department of Agriculture]. Those steps are already in place, and what we want to make sure is that you have first-hand knowledge, and not hearsay of the possible abuse.

Is [the bill] only targeting folks who deliberately seek employment for the purpose of taking undercover videos of possible animal abuse?

It's not targeting—this is all-inclusive, OK? What it's also saying is that this person is hired with the intent—the purpose—of going on, abusing animals, and filming it for their own personal gain, and that's what we don't want, because we just don't want that to happen.

What if there's a scenario where someone is just a regular employee with no ties to any animal welfare groups or anything like that, and they just see something happening that they don't feel is right. They're not sure, or they're worried about it, and they whip out their cell phone or something and they want to take some video or pictures so that they can document it, so that they can show law enforcement. What would happen in that case?

In that case right now I think it would be good for that person to go to the sheriff and say, "Hey, you know what? There is some abuse going on." And I don't care who they're connected with. If they see abuse, abuse is abuse. So what they need to do is go to the sheriff and say "Hey, there's some abuse going on here, or suspected abuse." And the sheriff says, "Go ahead, you take a picture and bring it back to me because you have first-hand knowledge."

Permission from Law Enforcement

OK, so you're saying that under this bill they would be required to go to law enforcement and get permission to take the images?

Mmm-hmm, mmm-hmm.

And otherwise, if they don't do that, if they're just there, and they're seeing something that they feel isn't right, and they want to just document it right then and there, and they take that video without having permission first, then is that something they could be prosecuted for?

Well, right now, what we're wanting to avoid is posting it on *YouTube* and hindering the process. Because if they would go to the law enforcement first, in other words, it is prescribed in law right now, that's the way they're supposed to do it, and we would like it to stay that way.

If somebody just happens to do something—you know, it's an "oops"—you know we all do oopsies—but if this is somebody you know is going to continually abuse the animals, you know, usually it isn't a one-time deal. And so if that person goes to the sheriff and says "Hey, this is what's going on—next day in, more than likely you know that's going to happen. We just want to make sure it's the proper channels and we don't want some kneejerk reaction to something that might not be what it appears.

I'm completely ignorant of legal stuff, but out of curiosity, would the sheriff have to get a court order, or a judge's permission for that kind of undercover video or photography?

No, not if the person works there. If the sheriff tells him to go ahead and take a picture the next day he's at work, and he brings it in with first-hand knowledge, that's fine.

So the sheriff has the authority to give that kind of permission.

Mmm-hmm.

> "History has shown that when workers do make complaints, they are often ignored or face job transfers, demotions, and other retaliatory actions."

Whistleblowers Help Protect National Food Supplies

Sarah Damian

Sarah Damian is a social and new media fellow for the Government Accountability Project, a whistleblower advocacy organization. In the following viewpoint, she argues that the agribusiness industry is attempting to silence whistleblowers. She points to legislation in Florida and Iowa that makes it illegal for individuals to make videos or take pictures on private farms. Damian argues that videos and pictures of health violations and animal rights abuses have in the past forced an end to dangerous and abusive practices.

As you read, consider the following questions:

1. What does Florida state Senator Jim Norman's bill do, according to Damian?

2. Who is Bradley Miller and what does he say about the anti-farm-video bill in Iowa?

3. What abuses at Food Lion grocery does Damian say that GAP uncovered?

When it comes to bringing horrific truths to the public eye, undercover footage and images are often an effective outlet for whistleblowers who otherwise risk retaliation when speaking up. Such use of media to promote transparency in our food system has come under attack, however, in recently proposed legislation.

Industry Targets Whistleblowers

Florida state Senator Jim Norman (R-Tampa) introduced a bill that criminalizes those who photograph farms without written consent of the owner, making the act a first-degree felony in Florida. Animal advocacy groups have fervently criticized the bill for "comparing a potential whistleblower who might expose the realities of factory farming . . . with those who commit murder or armed robbery." Rather than targeting the structures within Big Ag [Agriculture] that lead to violations such as inhumane handling and stifle workers' concerns regarding such violations, Senator Norman is attacking the efforts that threaten the industry's ability to keep them in place. The *Florida Independent* writes:

> There are currently no mechanisms in place to monitor animal welfare on Florida's farms, with inspections focusing on the food itself, not the conditions of the animals. Organizations such as PETA [People for the Ethical Treatment of Animals] and the Animal Rights Foundation of Florida contend Norman drafted the legislation in response to a number of high-profile exposés that revealed horrific conditions on farms around the country, and worry that without whistleblowers the industry will operate with impunity.

Whistleblower Intimidation by Agribusiness

For Tyson [Foods, a major agribusiness company] and other major firms, among the most damaging assertions [in the 1980s] were made by whistle-blowing federal inspectors, many of whom, like Vernon Gee, had lost their jobs for raising concerns about intimidation of inspectors by supervisors, along with widespread, willful skirting of safety guidelines. Gee, who worked at a Simmons [Foods] plant in southern Missouri, made a number of allegations, claiming that processing plants throughout the industry were rife with diseases, and that, among other violations, inspection reports were regularly falsified by co-opted inspectors; obviously contaminated meat was allowed to leave the plant en route to retail outlets; and inspectors were continually harassed until they became compliant with company production goals. Though Gee's affidavit didn't directly name Tyson (nor had he worked at a Tyson plant) his allegations nonetheless had a chilling effect on the company.

Brent E. Riffel, "The Feathered Kingdom:
Tyson Foods and the Transformation of
American Land, Labor, and Law, 1930–2005,"
PhD dissertation, University of Arkansas,
2008, p. 220.

Similarly, Iowa lawmakers are considering a bill that would make it illegal for animal rights activists to go undercover and record video of farm animal abuse. Associated Press reports:

Agriculture committees in the Iowa House and Senate have approved a bill that would prohibit such recordings and punish people who take agriculture jobs only to gain access to animals to record their treatment. Proposed penalties include fines of up to $7,500 and up to five years in prison. Votes by the full House and Senate have not yet been set.

The article quotes Bradley Miller, national director of the Humane Farming Association, who said that the bill is an attempt by agribusiness "to intimidate whistleblowers and put a chill on legitimate anti-cruelty investigations" and that the industry clearly "has something to hide or it wouldn't be going to these extreme and absurd lengths."

Since 1980, GAP [the Government Accountability Project] has worked with whistleblowers who, with the necessary help of undercover footage, were able to expose atrocious conditions that violated food integrity, and create change that benefited the animals, workers, and consumers.

Past Exposés

Past exposés include:

Chicken "Fecal Soup". USDA [US Department of Agriculture] grader Hobart Bartley, who was transferred and demoted in 1985 after repeatedly warning the agency of unsanitary conditions at a Missouri poultry plant, came to GAP and was able to expose the routine practice of soaking thousands of chicken carcasses in a giant "chiller" (with dried blood, feces and hair floating in along with the dead birds) in order to increase their selling weight, on CBS *60 Minutes.*

Food Lion. Food Lion grocery chain employees began to report to GAP shocking abuses of food safety standards in the early 1990s, such as grinding expired meat into sausage, washing off meat that was greenish and slimy, and soaking poultry in bleach to conceal spoilage. GAP took these concerns to ABC, which aired a national exposé on the confirmed allegations.

Dean Wyatt. Undercover footage taken by the Humane Society of the United States, and released in fall 2009, finally vindicated USDA Public Health Veterinarian Dean Wyatt, who consistently complained of animal welfare violations at two processing plants in Vermont and Oklahoma. Before the video's release, Wyatt lacked support from agency supervisors and was instead punished for doing his job.

History has shown that when workers *do* make complaints, they are often ignored or face job transfers, demotions, and other retaliatory actions that effectively (and unfortunately) discourage many from coming forward. Without the help of media and brave whistleblowers, these gross practices would go unchanged. It's a shame that introduced legislation in states like Iowa and Florida point fingers at the individuals we rely on to keep the safety and integrity of our food supply a priority, rather than reward their efforts and encourage their voices to be heard.

Periodical and Internet Sources Bibliography

The following articles have been selected to supplement the diverse views presented in this chapter.

Sandra Coliver	"National Security Whistleblowers: The Radical Dissenters of the 21st Century," *World Politics Review*, November 22, 2011. www.world politicsreview.com
Sarah Damian	"Hog Farm Whistleblower Proves Undercover Videos' Importance," *Food Integrity Campaign*, June 30, 2011. http://foodwhistleblower.org.
Andrew Duffelmeyer	"Ag Industry, Lawmakers Try to Limit Secret Videos," *ABC News*, March 14, 2011. http://abcnews .go.com.
Stephen M. Kohn	"The Whistle-Blowers of 1777," *New York Times*, June 12, 2011. www.nytimes.com.
New York Times	"Ex-Official for N.S.A. Accepts Deal in Leak Case," June 10, 2011. www.nytimes.com.
Will Potter	"Minnesota Bill Targets Anyone Who Exposes an 'Image or Sound' of Animals Suffering at Factory Farms, Puppy Mills," *Green Is the New Red*, April 6, 2011. www .greenisthenewred.com.
Alexandria Silver	"A Legal Assault on Animal-Abuse Whistle-Blowers?," *Time*, June 14, 2011. www.time.com.
David White	"Leaks and the Law: The Story of Thomas Drake," *Smithsonian.com*, August 2011. www.smithsonian mag.com.

OPPOSING
VIEWPOINTS®
SERIES

CHAPTER 3

Does WikiLeaks Perform a Valuable Function as a Whistleblower?

Chapter Preface

WikiLeaks, an international non-profit that publishes leaked documents from many sources, has sparked massive controversy. One of the claims made by its advocates is that it sparked the Arab Spring—the series of democratic revolutions that swept across the Middle East beginning in December 2010 and continuing as of December 2011.

In February 2010, WikiLeaks started to release more than 200,000 classified American diplomatic cables. These cables were communications sent to the US State Department by diplomats and embassy staffers. They included analysis of leaders and countries around the world. It was later alleged that the cables had been leaked by Bradley Manning, a US Army soldier.

Among the cables leaked by WikiLeaks were many in which US diplomats discussed the corruption of Tunisia's ruler, Zine el Abidine Ben Ali, and his family. For example, one cable said, "Whether it's cash, services, land, property, or yes, even your yacht, President Ben Ali's family is rumored to covet it and reportedly gets what it wants." Tunisians of course knew about the corruption of the ruling family. However, WikiLeaks, by providing specific information, helped to solidify opposition and hope, according to David Leigh and Luke Harding writing in a February 2, 2011, book extract in the *Guardian*. The protests in Tunisia were the beginning of the Arab Spring and ignited the wave of protests that swept across countries from Egypt to Libya.

Judy Bachrach, writing in a July–August 2011 article in *World Affairs*, argued that WikiLeaks also played a role in sparking rebellions beyond Tunisia. For example, Bachrach argues, revelations from WikiLeaks about Egypt President Hosni Mubarak's determination to stay in office helped to fire protests in that country. "In other words," Bachrach wrote, "the flames of revolt were stoked, industriously and ceaselessly, by the media, courtesy of what it was learning by sifting through piles of documents amassed by WikiLeaks."

WikiLeaks critics, however, have argued that its role in the Arab Spring has been exaggerated. Secretary of State Hillary Clinton's spokesperson Philip Crowley stated that "Tunisia is not a Wiki revolution. The Tunisian people knew about corruption long ago. They alone are the catalysts of this unfolding drama." Similarly, Jilian C. York, the director of international freedom of expression at the Electronic Frontier Foundation, stated in a January 14, 2011, post on her website that "By all Tunisian accounts, WikiLeaks had little—if anything—to do with the protests; rather, the protests were spurred by unemployment and economic woes. Furthermore, Tunisians have been documenting abuses by the Ben Ali regime and the first family for years."

The following chapter looks at arguments for and against the beneficial and harmful effects of WikiLeaks.

> "He [Bradley Manning] was ready to go to prison for life or even be executed, he said, in order to share this information with the American people who needed to have it."

WikiLeaks's Government Document Leaks Are Vital for Democracy

Daniel Ellsberg, interviewed by Brad Friedman

Daniel Ellsberg is a former US military analyst best known for releasing the Pentagon Papers, a secret Defense Department study of Vietnam, to the press. Brad Friedman is a blogger, journalist and radio broadcaster. In the following viewpoint, Ellsberg argues that secrecy is often more dangerous to US security than openness. He says that the WikiLeaks release of sensitive information was a brave and necessary act and gives Americans important information. He says that what WikiLeaks is doing is similar to what he did with the Pentagon Papers, and he believes it will make America more secure, not less.

As you read, consider the following questions:

1. What does Ellsberg say is his opinion of Bradley Manning, if it turns out that Manning provided the leaks to WikiLeaks?

2. Ellsberg says the Yemeni leader Selah was lying for the United States. What was he lying about, according to Ellsberg?

3. Why does Ellsberg say that Admiral Mullen is an expert on blood on hands?

Brad Friedman: Dan Ellsberg is the former military analyst who . . . brought the nation to a virtual standstill in 1971 when he released thousands of pages of top-secret documents to the New York Times *(and others) concerning U.S. Government involvement and decision making (in other words, lies) leading up to the Vietnam War, showing essentially that the [President Lyndon] Johnson Administration did lie to get us into that war. Those documents became known as the "Pentagon Papers" and their publication by the* Times *was challenged by the [Richard] Nixon Administration all the way up to the Supreme Court, after which Ellsberg was personally targeted by the Nixon Administration, a point which is interesting in light of the way that WikiLeaks [a non-profit international organization dedicated to publishing leaked documents] founder Julian Assange is now being targeted.*

Ellsberg has been a strong supporter of both WikiLeaks and Assange in the wake of the publication of hundreds of thousands of leaked documents from the Afghanistan and Iraq Wars (about which Dan Ellsberg says he has "waited 40 years for a release of documents on that scale"), and now hundred of thousands of cables sent to and from U.S. Embassy diplomats concerning our diplomatic efforts around the world.

He's also the subject of the 2009 Oscar-nominated documentary The Most Dangerous Man in America. *The most dangerous man in America now joins us on KPFK. Dan Ellsberg, welcome to the show, sir.*

Daniel Ellsberg: Glad to be here, Brad.

WikiLeaks and the Pentagon Papers

Delighted to talk to you. It's been awhile since we have talked. And we were talking at that time, a couple of years ago, about FBI whistleblower Sibel Edmonds. But let me just jump in right off the bat. You said that you've waited 40 years for a release of documents on this scale. I believe you were talking at the time about the Iraq war logs. Now we have this document dump, and that have been referred to even last night on The Daily Show, *as this generation's Pentagon Papers. Dan Ellsberg, how do you find that to be true and also how is it not true? In other words, how are these releases [different] from the Pentagon Papers back in 1971, as far as the information they have and the response to them from the media and the politicians?*

Sure, there are great differences as well as, I think, some very deep similarities; fundamentally similar in many ways. To start is of course that they mostly deal—not the latest ones, but the Afghan and the Iraq disclosures—deal with wars that are very similar to the war that was exposed in the Pentagon Papers. So many of the issues they reveal are very similar. And also they're both on a scale as to make the pursuit of the source of that very intense and probably successful. In my case I was sure they would know that I was the only, that I was the source of those, and so I expected to be put on trial. I expected, actually, to go to prison for the rest of my life. And the charges did add up to 115 years.

I'm very impressed that Bradley Manning, the suspect in this, who has not been proven to be the source yet by the Army but if the Army's—I should say the Pentagon and Army's suspicions are correct then I admire what he did and I feel a great affinity for it, because he did say, allegedly, to the person who turned him in, Adrian Lamo, in a chatlog, that he was prepared, he was ready to go to prison for life or even be executed, he said, in order to share this information with the American people who needed to have it. And that's the statement I said I've waited, in a way, for 40 years to hear someone make. I think it's an appropriate choice for somebody to make. It's not that they're obliged to be willing to do that so much. That's something a person has to decide for themselves very much. But I certainly think that when so many lives are at stake as in these wars or the new wars that may be coming at us, as in Yemen or even Pakistan, that to try to avert those is appropriate and to shorten them when they're clearly hopeless and dangerous, as in Afghanistan.

Well, Dan, is there a difference. . . .

It's worth one's own life to try to avert that.

Is there a difference in the documents that were released allegedly by Bradley Manning in that they concerned an ongoing hot war, so to speak, and documents that could endanger people out in the field right now versus the largely historical documents of the Pentagon Papers that looked back over several decades.

Look, to start with, yes, they are a different level of government bureaucratic communication here. These are, both the Afghan and Iraq logs, are field level, in those cases military—pretty much—communications of the kind that lie behind the Pentagon Papers, but the Pentagon Papers were high level, top secret decision papers that showed a great warning, actually, about the escalations that lay ahead, as well as planning for escalations that was being concealed from the American public. Wrongly, I would say, leading them into very dangerous, reckless policies. So these are not the Pentagon Papers. Unfortunately. I wish they were. We need the Pentagon Papers, not only of Afghanistan and

Iraq, but as I said, of Yemen, Pakistan and other wars that may lie, or actually covertly . . .

Well, that we find that we're now in, Dan! You know . . .

Covert stage.

Right.

Yemen, Secrecy, and Lies

Less so in Pakistan but very much in Yemen. One of these cases, of course, reveals that the Yemeni leaders, [President Ali Abdullah] Saleh and his deputy and so forth, are assuring. [General David] Petraeus that they were lying for us and lying to keep it from their own people that Yemen was being bombed by a foreign power, namely us. And of course that's keeping it from the American people as well. We weren't admitting that. And not only to keep it from the Yemeni people but to keep it from Americans because Americans, I think, do have a right to know who we're bombing, who we're at war with. Certainly Congress should be making that decision and has not been. Certainly. So our Constitution is being absolutely flouted on that, as is true in Iraq, for example. Or in Vietnam. So there have been some significant revelations, although on the whole these latest releases, large as they are in scale, haven't yet proven as informative as the earlier ones on Afghan and Iraq. And they're not, as I say, at the level of the Pentagon Papers. I wish they were. And yet there have been a number of significant revelations there. I mentioned one, that we were bombing . . .

Yemen, certainly. Yeah.

. . . and that that was being concealed for us by lies to the Yemeni Parliament, which amount to lies by us, as well, to our own people. But another example, for instance, which is rather like some

A Pentagon Papers of the Middle East

Many high-level officers and government officials are convinced that our president [George W. Bush] will attempt to bring about regime change in Iran by air attack; that he and his vice president [Dick Cheney] have long been no less committed, secretly, to doing so than they were to attacking Iraq. . .

Simply resigning in silence does not meet moral or political responsibilities of officials rightly "appalled" by the thrust of secret policy. I hope that one or more such persons will make the sober decision—accepting sacrifice of clearance and career, and risk of prison—to disclose comprehensive files that convey, irrefutably, official, secret estimates of costs and prospects and dangers of the military plans being considered. What needs disclosure is the full internal controversy, the secret critiques as well as the arguments and claims of advocates of war and nuclear "options"—the Pentagon Papers [which uncovered information on the Vietnam War] of the Middle East.

Daniel Ellsberg, "The Nest War," Harper's,
October 2006. http://harpers.org.

of the things in the Pentagon Papers, were the warnings by our former or recent ambassador to Pakistan, Anne Patterson, that our policy there of bombing, drone attacks and other attacks in Pakistan was, as she put it, counterproductive and dangerous. Meaning that it's endangering a regime that, with all its faults, Pakistan, is less bad for us in the world and for Pakistan than what might well follow it if we destabilize it. And what we're doing is destabilizing that regime. What that also means is that our policies . . . in both Yemen and Pakistan, and Afghanistan, are endangering Americans at home. The idea that these releases are dangerous I think conceals a very misleading and basically dangerous attitude. And that is that the only risks to Americans lie in telling the truth or exposing these operations, or in any degree of transparency. Now, there may be some risks, in some cases. There are risks in democracy, and there's risks in openness. It's not without any risk. Our Constitution, on the whole, relies on our taking those risks in order to be a democracy and to have, to avoid debacles like the ones we've just been mentioning. But what these critics don't seem to recognize is that our current debacles in Afghanistan, Iraq, Pakistan, Yemen, all these places, do not result from too much openness or too much transparency. They reflect the risks which were realized risks having to do with secrecy and silence and lies. The silence about the lies that got us into Iraq, for example, or, and in general the decision-making that is getting us into these. Now, the case of Yemen, for example. Probably there are, there's an argument to be made about whether we should be attacking supposedly Al-Qaeda cells in Yemen. At the same time, many people in the government, it has been leaked now, actually believe that those attacks will mainly be targeted with the help of Saleh, the ruler in Yemen, against people who have no relation to Al-Qaeda, people are opposing his regime for various good or bad reasons.

And indeed there have been a huge amount of civilian deaths, we now learn, in . . .

Not only civilian deaths but also the people they're actually targeting had to do with civil wars, a separatist movement in the south, rebels in the north, that have nothing to do with Al-Qaeda and nothing to do with the United States.

MERCY MALICK (News Director): So we may be targeting political opponents. . . .

What Should Not Be Leaked

FRIEDMAN: Is there anything, Dan Ellsberg, is there anything that should not be leaked because it really does pose a risk to national security? Is that any excuse at all for not releasing this classified information, because it might put someone at risk?

Well, yes. Sure, there could be. For example, but we have some experience on that now, as to whether these particular releases actually show that risk, or show the danger. The risk is there. In the initial releases it was alleged that there were the names of informants to the United States which should not have been released. Although, in fact, a number had been redacted already by WikiLeaks as well as by the newspapers. And so we were told by Admiral [Michael] Mullen and others that surely people had already been killed as a result of this and many more would be. Well, six months have passed since the Pentagon first got the contents, in this case, of Bradley Manning's computer, and then they were released a couple of months later. And the Pentagon itself has acknowledged that they have no evidence that any single person has been harmed as a result of that. In fact, they went further, rather surprisingly, in Kabul [Afghanistan], to say that they hadn't found it necessary after all to inform or protect any one of those individuals. So if there was a risk there, fortunately no one was harmed.

On the other hand, and since then, WikiLeaks and the newspapers have gone to much greater lengths now to redact the names, and if there was no harm from the first results I think there's no reason at all to expect it in this case. On the other hand, Admiral Mullen is something of an expert, I guess, on blood on hands, because he's one of the people who has sent these troops into harm's way in wars they should not be pursuing or escalating at this time. And that's not just a risk. Thousands of Americans have died as a result of that. And I would say, from what I was saying earlier, Americans at home have definitely been endangered by the help that these operations give to Al-Qaeda, who is a genuine enemy of ours. They recruit for Al-Qaeda. They make it hard for other countries, whether they're democracies or in most cases not democracies, countries whose cooperation we need against possible terrorists in their country, make it hard for them to help us. They have to do it secretly.

And that's what we have . . .

That's why any cooperation with the U.S. is so unpopular, and that reflects the fact that our presidents have chosen to bomb those countries.

And that's one of the things that we have learned from these leaks, that in fact a lot of this ends up being a recruitment opportunity for Al-Qaeda. Speaking with whistleblower, Pentagon Papers whistle-blower Daniel Ellsberg. Dan, you wrote an op ed at The BRAD BLOG, what was it, February 2008, you said, "Many if not most covert operations deserve to be disclosed by a free press. They are often covert not only because they are illegal but because they are wildly ill-conceived and reckless. . . . Sensitive and covert are syn-onymous for half-assed, idiotic and dangerous to national security as well as criminal."

"All panelists saw great risk in leaking vast amounts of secret information with no apparent or coherent cause, other than the desire to embarrass government officials."

WikiLeaks's Government Document Leaks Are a Danger to Democracy

CIGI

Centre for International Governance Innovation (CIGI) is an independent, non-partisan think tank on international governance. In the following viewpoint, CIGI describes a panel discussion about WikiLeaks. The panelists concluded that openness and transparency were important and that leaks were sometimes justified. However, they argued that WikiLeaks's massive leak of government documents would cause a reduction in openness and could cause harm to individuals as well. They concluded that leaks should be more carefully regulated and controlled.

As you read, consider the following questions:

1. In what ways does Paul Heinbecker believe WikiLeaks will result in less, rather than more, openness?

2. In what ways does Andrew Hunt say that WikiLeaks differs from the Pentagon Papers?

3. According to Geoffrey Stevens, what is the journalistic bias with which he approached the issue of WikiLeaks?

W histle-blowers are vital to the democratic process, but the wholesale and indiscriminate leak of government secrets is a danger to democracy, a public panel discussion on the WikiLeaks controversy has concluded.

WikiLeaks Will Reduce Openness

WikiLeaks, a not-for-profit group created in 2006, is an intermediary for whistleblowers to divulge secret documents; and last year [2010], it posted thousands of secret U.S. diplomatic cables to its website. Meanwhile, its founder, Julian Assange, is currently fighting unrelated sex assault charges involving relationships he had in Sweden.

The impact of the leaked diplomatic memos was discussed by a panel of experts at The Centre for International Governance Innovation (CIGI), in Waterloo on January 12, 2011—a public event attended by 270 people and also webcast live to a global audience.

Participants were: Paul Heinbecker, a CIGI Distinguished Fellow, former ambassador and permanent representative of Canada to the United Nations; Andrew Hunt, an associate professor of history at the University of Waterloo; Mark McArdle, a Waterloo-based technology executive and CEO [chief executive officer] of tinyHippos; and moderator Geoffrey Stevens, an author, teacher and journalist.

"Process" and "substance," Heinbecker explained in his opening remarks, will be the diplomatic consequences of WikiLeaks. "The net result of this effort to open up the system will be to close it," he added as he expressed concern that diplomats worldwide may in future put fewer thoughts into writing, possibly express-

ing their confidential opinions to their governments through secure satellite-links or in person. "What you'll end up with is not
an access to information regime that works for everybody. . . .
What you'll end up with is people stopping to put things down
in records." This could, in the longer-term, deprive citizens and
historians of significant diplomatic records.

Heinbecker also warned that tighter internal controls within
governments on who has access to documents might lead to
more silos among departments and agencies, and inhibit the increased information-sharing that occurred to help combat terrorism after the 9/11 [2001] attacks.

As he referenced the case of former Timor-Leste diplomat
Scott Gilmore, Heinbecker also warned of the danger which
WikiLeaks could have on sources of information. "[Gilmore]
was meeting with human rights advocates at a time when it was
extremely dangerous [and] they were giving him evidence of
crimes that had been committed against human rights activists.
How could he continue to do that if . . . his interlocutor thought
that the next day this could be revealed in a cable that might
end up on the front page of a newspaper? It's a bit like being a
journalist—the source is going to dry up."

WikiLeaks and the Pentagon Papers

Hunt took a historical view, comparing WikiLeaks to the case
of Daniel Ellsberg, who in the early 1970s famously leaked the
Pentagon Papers that revealed U.S. government lies about the
Vietnam War. The two episodes have both similarities and striking differences, Hunt noted. Ellsberg was a patriot, motivated
by his belief to reveal what he saw as an un-American activity
being committed by the powerful; and his efforts to disclose a
single-issue leak required two years of laborious low-tech pho-
tocopying with the engagement of mass media to deliver the
news. In contrast, Assange has general discontent aimed at the
U.S. government, uses high-technology that does not require
mass media involvement, and takes a scattergun approach that

The Problem with WikiLeaks

The real problem with WikiLeaks [WL] is that it tried to do too many things at once. WL encompassed the entire whistle-blowing process. The sources uploaded the documents; WL members erased the metadata, verified the submissions, and provided the context in additional texts. In the end, everything was put on the WL site.

At some point, it became impossible to do all these jobs adequately. There were simply too many documents coming in. That would have taken hundreds of deeply involved volunteers. So we were compelled to make choices. Which leaks should see the light of day, and which ones would lie unpublished on servers spread across the world? We were overwhelmed.

Daniel Domscheit-Berg and Tina Klopp,
Inside Wikileaks: My Time with Julian
Assange at the World's Most Dangerous
Website, *trans. Jefferson Chase. New York, NY:*
Crown Publishers, 2011, p. 269.

leaks information on a vast range of issues. "This will take quite some time—to make sense of these documents," Hunt said of the WikiLeak cables.

Both men were publicly vilified in their time, and yet time has come to vindicate Ellsberg, now seen as having helped improve American government in his day. "We still have to verify [their] veracity" and "it remains to be seen what history's verdict on some many of these [Wikileak] documents will be," Hunt explained.

Contemplating the validity of WikiLeaks as an important and valuable whistleblower, McArdle pointed out that while it raises serious issues for international relations and diplomacy, the same publication model and technology approach deployed by Assange are privacy concerns for every business, every family, and every individual. Given the scale of enterprise data that was released, "I think it sheds a light on how technology comes to bear on how we manage assets," McArdle said. "Technology has made everyone in this room potentially a publisher and anyone who finds something they think is intriguing is just minutes away from publishing it to the world."

The important lesson of WikiLeaks for governments, brought up by McArdle, include the necessity to manage, through technology, how information is accessed, searched and distributed. If a single individual was able to download 260,000 secret documents—as may have happened in the transmission of U.S. diplomatic cables from a former American soldier to WikiLeaks—perhaps that should have set off certain internal alarms.

Serving as moderator, Stevens declared his journalistic bias at the outset of the discussion in favour of government transparency. "I believe that government which gathers information at the taxpayers' expense should make that information available to the public . . . unless there is some compelling reason why it should not be," he said. He recounted his experiences as a journalist with anecdotes about the federal sponsorship scandal and the need for open access to government information.

Great Risks

Stevens concluded the evening event by summarizing the views of the panellists, who all acknowledged that a discriminating leak of information, by well-intentioned people, to reveal wrong doing may be justifiable and even highly desirable—the *Pentagon Papers* were such a case. At the same time, all panellists saw great risk in leaking vast amounts of secret information with no apparent or coherent cause, other than the desire to embarrass government officials. Such risks include new controls that might further inhibit access to information, damage international relations, and even cause injury or death to innocent individuals involved in important secret missions. Technology makes this possible, but the impact on global governance—and on ordinary lives— has yet to be fully evaluated.

During a question-and-answer session, panel participants took questions not only from the audience present in the CIGI Atrium in Waterloo, but also questions posted by email from the global webcast audience, which included viewers in Mexico, Florida and also various communities in Canada. As part of its strategy for global outreach, CIGI intends to webcast most or all of its public events in future.

"For bringing us the truth, for breaking the seal on that self-protective policy of secrecy, Bradley Manning deserves the Presidential Medal of Freedom."

Alleged WikiLeaks Whistleblower Bradley Manning Is a Hero

Chase Madar

Chase Madar is a lawyer and the author of The Passion of Bradley Manning. *In the following viewpoint, he argues that if Bradley Manning did provide WikiLeaks with leaked government documents, then he should receive the Presidential Medal of Freedom. Madar says that the leaks, allegedly by Manning, held the American government accountable, helped to encourage democracy in the Middle East, exposed over-classification of government documents, and advanced the goal of transparency.*

As you read, consider the following questions:

1. Who is Robert Gates, and why does Madar suggest he does not deserve the Presidential Medal of Freedom more than Bradley Manning?

2. Why does Madar say that Manning was responsible for democratic revolutions in the Middle East?

3. Who is Barton J. Bernstein and how did he characterize the government's classification of foreign-policy documents?

W e still don't know if he did it or not, but if Bradley Manning, the 24-year-old Army private from Oklahoma, actually supplied WikiLeaks with its choicest material—the Iraq War logs, the Afghan War logs, and the State Department cables—which startled and riveted the world, then he deserves the Presidential Medal of Freedom instead of a jail cell at Fort Leavenworth.[1]

A Medal, Not a Court Martial

President [Barack] Obama recently gave one of those medals to retiring Secretary of Defense Robert Gates, who managed the two bloody, disastrous wars about which the WikiLeaks-released documents revealed so much. Is he really more deserving than the young private who, after almost ten years of mayhem and catastrophe, gave Americans—and the world—a far fuller sense of what our government is actually doing abroad?

Bradley Manning, awaiting a court martial in December [2011], faces the prospect of long years in prison. He is charged with violating the Espionage Act of 1917. He has put his sanity and his freedom on the line so that Americans might know what our government has done—and is still doing—globally. He has blown the whistle on criminal violations of American military law. He has exposed our secretive government's pathological over-classification of important public documents.

Here are four compelling reasons why, if he did what the government accuses him of doing, he deserves that medal, not jail time.

Supervision, a Public Responsibility

At great personal cost, Bradley Manning has given our foreign policy elite the public supervision it so badly needs. In the past 10 years,

American statecraft has moved from calamity to catastrophe, laying waste to other nations while never failing to damage our own national interests. Do we even need to be reminded that our self-defeating response to 9/11 [2001], in Iraq and Afghanistan (and Pakistan, Yemen, and Somalia) has killed roughly 225,000 civilians and 6,000 American soldiers, while costing our country more than $3.2 trillion? We are hemorrhaging blood and money. Few outside Washington [D.C.] would argue that any of this is making America safer.

An employee who screwed up this badly would either be fired on the spot or put under heavy supervision. Downsizing our entire foreign policy establishment is not an option. However, the website WikiLeaks has at least tried to make public scrutiny of our self-destructive statesmen and -women a reality by exposing their work to ordinary citizens.

Consider our invasion of Iraq, a war based on distortions, government secrecy, and the complaisant failure of our major media to ask the important questions. But what if someone like Bradley Manning had provided the press with the necessary government documents, which would have made so much self-evident in the months before the war began? Might this not have prevented disaster? We'll never know, of course, but could additional public scrutiny have been salutary under the circumstances?

Thanks to Bradley Manning's alleged disclosures, we do have a sense of what did happen afterwards in Iraq and Afghanistan, and just how the U.S. operates in the world. Thanks to those disclosures, we now know just how Washington leaned on the Vatican to quell opposition to the Iraq War and just how it pressured the Germans to prevent them from prosecuting CIA agents who kidnapped an innocent man and shipped him off to be tortured abroad.

As our foreign policy threatens to careen into yet more disasters in Yemen, Pakistan, Somalia, and Libya, we can only hope that more whistleblowers will follow the alleged example of Bradley Manning and release vital public documents before it's too late. A foreign policy based on secrets and spin has manifestly failed us. In a democracy, the workings of our government should not be shrouded in an opaque cloud of secrecy. For bringing us the truth, for breaking the seal on that self-protective policy of secrecy, Bradley Manning deserves the Presidential Medal of Freedom.

Knowledge and Democracy

Knowledge is powerful. The WikiLeaks disclosures have helped spark democratic revolutions and reforms across the Middle East, accomplishing what Operation Iraqi Freedom never could. Wasn't it American policy to spread democracy in the Middle East, to extend our freedom to others, as both recent American presidents have insisted?

No single American has done more to help further this goal than Pfc. [private first class] Bradley Manning. The chain reaction of democratic protests and uprisings that has swept Egypt, Libya, Bahrain, Syria, Yemen, and even in a modest way Iraq, all began in Tunisia, where leaked U.S. State Department cables about the staggering corruption of the ruling Ben Ali dynasty helped trigger the rebellion. In all cases, these societies were smoldering with longstanding grievances against oppressive, incompetent governments and economies stifled by cronyism. The revelations from the WikiLeaks State Department documents played a widely acknowledged role in sparking these pro-democracy uprisings.

In Egypt, Tunisia, Bahrain, and Yemen, the people's revolts under way have occurred despite U.S. support for their autocratic rulers. In each of these nations, in fact, we bankrolled the dictators, while helping to arm and train their militaries. The alliance with [President of Egypt Hosni] Mubarak's autocratic state cost the U.S. more than $60 billion and did nothing for American security—other than inspire terrorist blowback from radicalized Egyptians like Mohammad Atta and Ayman al-Zawahiri.

Even if U.S. policy was firmly on the wrong side of things, we should be proud that at least one American—Bradley Manning—

was on the right side. If indeed he gave those documents to WikiLeaks, then he played a catalytic role in bringing about the Arab Spring, something neither Barack Obama nor former Secretary of Defense Robert Gates (that recent surprise recipient of the Presidential Medal of Freedom) could claim. Perhaps once the Egyptians consolidate their democracy, they, too, will award Manning their equivalent of such a medal.

Over-Classification

Bradley Manning has exposed the pathological over-classification of America's public documents. "Secrecy is for losers," as the late Senator and United Nations Ambassador Daniel Patrick Moynihan used to say. If this is indeed the case, it would be hard to find a bigger loser than the U.S. government.

How pathological is our government's addiction to secrecy? In June, the National Security Agency declassified documents from 1809, while the Department of Defense only last month declassified the Pentagon Papers, publicly available in book form these last four decades. Our government is only just now finishing its declassification of documents relating to World War I.

This would be ridiculous if it weren't tragic. Ask the historians. Barton J. Bernstein, professor emeritus of history at Stanford University and a founder of its international relations program, describes the government's classification of foreign-policy documents as "bizarre, arbitrary, and nonsensical." George Herring, professor emeritus at the University of Kentucky and author of the encyclopedic *From Colony to Superpower: A History of U.S. Foreign Policy*, has chronicled how his delight at being appointed to a CIA advisory panel on declassification turned to disgust once he realized that he was being used as window dressing by an agency with no intention of opening its records, no matter how important or how old, to public scrutiny.

Any historian worth his salt would warn us that such over-classification is a leading cause of national amnesia and repetitive war disorder. If a society like ours doesn't know its own history, it becomes the great power equivalent of an itinerant amnesiac, not knowing what it did yesterday or where it will end up tomorrow. Right now, classification is the disease of Washington, secrecy its mania, and dementia its end point. As an ostensibly democratic nation, we, its citizens, risk such ignorance at our national peril.

President Obama came into office promising a "sunshine" policy for his administration while singing the praises of whistleblowers. He has since launched the fiercest campaign against whistleblowers the republic has ever seen, and further plunged our foreign policy into the shadows. Challenging the classification of each tightly guarded document is, however, impossible. No organization has the resources to fight this fight, nor would they be likely to win right now. Absent a radical change in our government's diplomatic and military bureaucracies, massive over-classification will only continue.

If we hope to know what our government is actually doing in our name globally, we need massive leaks from insider whistleblowers to journalists who can then sort out what we need to know, given that the government won't. This, in fact, has been the modus operandi of WikiLeaks. Our whistleblower protection laws urgently need to catch up to this state of affairs, and though we are hardly there yet, Bradley Manning helped take us part of the way. He did what Barack Obama swore he would do on coming into office. For striking a blow against our government's fanatical insistence on covering its mistakes and errors with blanket secrecy, Bradley Manning deserves not punishment, but the Presidential Medal of Freedom.

Transparency Is an American Tradition

At immense personal cost, Bradley Manning has upheld a great American tradition of transparency in statecraft and for that he should be an American hero, not an American felon. Bradley Manning is only the latest in a long line of whistleblowers in and

out of uniform who have risked everything to put our country back on the right path.

Take Daniel Ellsberg, leaker of the Pentagon Papers, a Pentagon-commissioned secret history of the Vietnam War and the official lies and distortions that the government used to sell it. Many of the documents it included were classed at a much higher security clearance than anything Bradley Manning is accused of releasing—and yet Ellsberg was not convicted of a single crime and became a national hero.

Given the era when all this went down, it's forgivable to assume that Ellsberg must have been a hippie who somehow sneaked into the Pentagon archives, beads and patchouli trailing behind him. What many no longer realize is that Ellsberg had been a model U.S. Marine. First in his class at officer training school at Quantico, he deferred graduate school at Harvard to remain on active duty in the Marine Corps. Ellsberg saw his high-risk exposure of the disastrous and deceitful nature of the Vietnam War as fully consonant with his long career of patriotic service in and out of uniform.

And Ellsberg is hardly alone. Ask Lt. Colonel (ret.) Darrel Vandeveld [involved in the prosecution of a suspected terrorist]. Or Tom Drake, formerly of the National Security Agency.

Transparency in statecraft was not invented last week by WikiLeaks creator Julian Assange. It is a longstanding American tradition. [Former President] James Madison put the matter succinctly: "A popular government, without popular information, or the means of acquiring it, is but a prologue to a farce or a tragedy; or, perhaps both."

A 1960 Congressional Committee on Government Operations report caught the same spirit: "Secrecy—the first refuge of incompetents—must be at a bare minimum in a democratic society. . . . Those elected or appointed to positions of executive authority must recognize that government, in a democracy, cannot be wiser than the people." John F. Kennedy made the same point in 1961: "The very word 'secrecy' is repugnant in a free and open society." Hugo Black, great Alabaman justice of the twentieth-century Supreme Court had this to say: "The guarding of military and diplomatic secrets at the expense of informed representative government provides no real security for our Republic." And the first of World-War-I-era president Woodrow Wilson's 14 Points couldn't have been more explicit: "*Open covenants of peace, openly arrived at*, after which there shall be no private international understandings of any kind but *diplomacy shall proceed always frankly and in the public view.*"

We need to know what our government's commitments are, as our foreign policy elites have clearly demonstrated they cannot be left to their own devices. Based on the last decade of carnage and folly, without public debate—and aggressive media investigations—we have every reason to expect more of the same.

If there's anything to learn from that decade, it's that government secrecy and lies come at a very high price in blood and money. Thanks to the whistleblowing revelations attributed to Bradley Manning, we at least have a far clearer picture of the problems we face in trying to supervise our own government. If he was the one responsible for the WikiLeaks revelations, then for his gift to the republic, purchased at great price, he deserves not prison, but a Presidential Medal of Freedom and the heartfelt gratitude of his country.

Note

1. In 2010, WikiLeaks released leaked, secret US documents pertaining to the US war in Iraq and the US war in Afghanistan. It also released secret US diplomatic cables.

> *"If found guilty [Bradley Manning and Julian Assange] deserve nothing less than death sentences for their unspeakable crimes."*

WikiLeaks Whistleblowers Are Traitors

Michael Reagan

Michael Reagan is a political consultant and the son of former President Ronald Reagan. In the following viewpoint, he argues that Bradley Manning, who allegedly leaked classified US documents, and Julian Assange, the editor of WikiLeaks who published them, both deserve to be prosecuted and executed. Reagan says that publishing classified information in wartime amounts to treason or espionage and will seriously damage America. He adds that media outlets that published the classified information should also be prosecuted.

As you read, consider the following questions:

1. What example of a secret operation does Reagan use to illustrate his argument that some secrets should not be shared with the public?

2. What law does Reagan say Julian Assange may have violated?

3. Why does the Justice Department think it would be difficult to prosecute media organizations that published WikiLeaks documents, according to Reagan?

If we had a president in the White House [that is, someone other than President Barack Obama] who understood that we are at war with a crazed faction of Islam, and was willing to act on that belief, there would be no question about how we should deal with people who give aid and comfort to the enemy—they'd be tried for treason and when found guilty stood up before a firing squad.

Betrayal

Julian Assange [the editor-in-chief of WikiLeaks] and his fellow conspirator Pvt. Bradley Manning [an Army soldier who allegedly gave classified documents to WikiLeaks] allegedly betrayed the United States, gave aid and comfort to the terrorists who seek to destroy the United States, and if found guilty they deserve nothing less than death sentences for their unspeakable crimes.

Their pitifully lame excuse that they were merely trying to provide information to the American people that was being improperly withheld from them by the government is on a par with Benedict Arnold's claim that he was merely trying to inform the British on information the American people believed they deserved to have.

On the contrary, the public does not have the right to know everything—some information needs to be kept secret if the public's safety is to be assured. Consumers do not need to know the gory details of how sausage is made, nor do the people need to be made aware of all of the details of what is being done to protect them.

Nobody ever demanded that those scientists engaged in building the atomic bomb that ended the war with Japan should do their work openly and share their secrets with the public, and nobody has the right to decide which secrets the public has a need to know.

The release of these so-called WikiLeaks documents has put the American people at risk, as Secretary of State [Hillary] Clinton has said, and the two culprits deserve to be made to pay the price for their treasonous actions.

Pvt. Bradley Manning, the soldier who is alleged to have illegally obtained the documents, is already behind bars where, if justice is to be served, he will remain for the rest of his life.

Assange's punishment is yet to be determined, but it should be equally as harsh, if indeed he escapes the hangman's noose, although he should not.

A Dagger in the Heart

According to news reports, the Feds are attempting to learn whether Assange violated any criminal laws, most notably those covered under the Espionage Act.

Both the [Department of] Justice (DOJ) and Defense Departments say they are conducting "an active ongoing criminal investigation" of the entire matter, but there is no question of the serious nature of the crimes committed by Assange and Manning—by their despicable actions they have plunged a dagger into the hearts of the American people.

Moreover, the FBI is currently looking into the activities of all those who had come into possession of the subject documents, especially those who provided secret information to Assange's WikiLeaks organization. If they are found to be culpable they should be harshly punished.

There are problems involved in prosecuting the two men. Legal experts warn that prosecuting those charged with illegally leaking classified documents is difficult for a number of reasons, not the least being persuading foreign governments to hand Assange—who lives abroad—over to U.S. prosecutors.

It should be kept in mind that Assange and Manning are not the only entities who have put the American people at risk. Those in the media who couldn't wait to publish the information given them by the pair are equally guilty of endangering the American people.

Indeed, it has been reported that DOJ is warning that media organizations could well be subject to prosecution, although that is said not to be in the cards because Justice fears possible violations of the First Amendment, and is fully aware that it has never prosecuted such a matter.

According to Kenneth Wainstein, former assistant attorney general in the national security division, "Whenever you're talking about a media organization, the department is going to look very closely to ensure that any prosecution doesn't undermine the valid First Amendment functioning of the press."

Jeffrey H. Smith, a former CIA general counsel, noted that Assange is the DOJ's target. "I'm confident that the Justice Department is figuring out how to prosecute him," Smith told reporters.

They need to go further than that.

They need to be figuring out how to hang him.

Periodical and Internet Sources Bibliography

The following articles have been selected to supplement the diverse views presented in this chapter.

Andrew Cohen	"Patriot or Traitor?: Views on Bradley Manning's Treatment Differ," *Atlantic*, March 17, 2011. www.theatlantic.com.
Noam Cohen	"Web Attackers Find a Rallying Cry in WikiLeaks," *New York Times*, December 9, 2010. www.nytimes.com.
The Economist	"Business and Wikileaks: Be Afraid," December 9, 2010. www.economist.com.
Barton Gellman	"Person of the Year 2010: Runners-Up: Julian Assange," *Time*, December 15, 2010. www.time.com.
Glenn Greenwald	"The Motives of Bradley Manning," *Salon*, July 4, 2011. www.salon.com.
Evan Hansen	"Is Bradley Manning a Traitor Or a Hero?," *Huffington Post*, July 14, 2011. www.huffingtonpost.com.
Doug Mataconis	"State Department: Wikileaks Did Not Cause Any Lasting Damage," *Outside the Beltway*, January 19, 2011. www.outsidethebeltway.com.
Noam Scheiber	"Game Changer," *New Republic*, December 27, 2010. www.tnr.com.
Peter Tatchell	"One Year in Jail, Bradley Manning Is a Hero," *New Statesman*, May 18, 2011. www.newstatesman.com.
Sid Yadav	"PayPal Follows Anti-Wikileaks Crusade, Suspends Account," VentureBeat.com, December 4, 2010. http://venturebeat.com.

OPPOSING
VIEWPOINTS®
SERIES

CHAPTER 4

What Consequences Do Whistleblowers Face?

Chapter Preface

Karen Silkwood was a chemical technician at the Kerr-McGee nuclear power plant near Crescent, Oklahoma. She was a union organizer and a whistleblower who publicly charged the plant with maintaining unsafe conditions for its workers. Some have argued that her whistleblowing resulted in violent reprisals and ultimately led to her death.

Silkwood was elected by her union local in the early 1970s to investigate health and safety issues at the Kerr-McGee plant. She found many instances of what she believed to be violations of safety standards. Among other problems, samples were stored incorrectly and there were insufficient showers. Silkwood was concerned that workers might become contaminated. In 1974 she testified on problems in the plant before the Atomic Energy Commission. Following her testimony, Silkwood discovered that she had been contaminated with a massive overdose of plutonium. She believed that she had been exposed in retaliation for her whistleblowing.

Despite her fears for her own safety, Silkwood continued to investigate the Kerr-McGee plant. According to Silkwood's mother, "Every night she called scared and crying. . . . She thought she was dying. I told her to quit and come home, but she felt she had to stay and clean that plant up," as quoted in Linda Witt's June 4, 1979, article in *People*.

Silkwood arranged to meet with a *New York Times* reporter to turn over documents allegedly outlining Kerr-McGhee's safety violations. En route to the meeting, her car ran off the road and she was killed. No documents were found in the car, and there was speculation that she had been deliberately murdered to prevent her from talking to the press. An autopsy showed that Silkwood "had probably been exposed [to plutonium] within 30 days prior to her death," according to a report published in *Los Alamos Science* on November 23, 1995.

Silkwood's family sued the Kerr-McGhee plant, arguing that the plant's negligence had caused Silkwood's contamination. Kerr-McGhee argued that Silkwood had deliberately contaminated herself. The jury rejected that argument and in 1979 awarded the family $10.5 million in damages. That amount was thrown out on appeal, and eventually Kerr-McGhee settled out of court for $1.38 million. The exact cause of Silkwood's death and of her plutonium exposure remains a mystery.

The following viewpoints look at instances of retaliation for whistleblowing.

"Even good organizations, managed by honest and decent leaders, may engage in the most determined and contemptible reprisals."

Organizations Often Defend Themselves by Attacking Whistleblowers

David Hutton

David Hutton is the executive director of FAIR, a Canadian charity dedicated to the protection of whistleblowers. In the following viewpoint, he says that whistleblowers often face severe retaliation from their organizations or companies. He argues that companies often attack whistleblowers' reputations and livelihoods and that the legal system does little to stop them. Wrongdoers, on the other hand, often get off with no penalty or with generous severance packages, Hutton argues. He concludes that Canadians can change this by pushing for government action and better laws.

As you read, consider the following questions:

1. Who is Christiane Ouimet, and how does Hutton say she treated whistleblowers and wrongdoers?
2. What trump cards are held by wrongdoers within management ranks, according to Hutton?
3. Why does Hutton say that people guilty of blatant misconduct often receive soft landings?

Former integrity commissioner Christiane Ouimet's testimony to the [Canadian] House Public Accounts Committee seemed to be all about her: how she was victimized by the auditor general's intensive investigation; how she was forced out of office (with a $500,000 payoff); the damage done to her reputation and her health; and the interruption of her vacation to appear before the committee.

Whistleblowers and Wrongdoers

Virtually absent from the discussion were two very important groups of people: the whistleblowers whose cases were routinely rejected under Ouimet's leadership; and the alleged wrongdoers who she so effectively shielded from investigation.

At the meeting we caught glimpses of some whistleblowers. We saw former Transport Canada inspector Hugh Danford angrily berating Ouimet as she strode impassively from the committee room. Danford confessed tearfully afterwards to CBC's [Canadian Broadcast Corporation's] Laurie Graham how his life has been destroyed, "Look at me: I used to be a pilot. Would you want to fly with me?" Danford had tried to alert Transport Canada to systemic safety issues.

Also present were Dr. Shiv Chopra and his colleague Dr. Margaret Haydon—scientists who exposed how Health Canada pressured them to release inadequately tested drugs into the food supply. Sean Bruyea was there too, the former Gulf War intelligence officer who became a vocal advocate on behalf of wounded veterans whose benefits were being slashed. All of these people suffered severe reprisals for their dedication to the public interest. All tried to get help from Ouimet's office and were rebuffed. All wanted to hear what she had to say for herself.

But it's the other group of unrepresented people that I want to focus on: the alleged wrongdoers. Some may be innocent, but others may be found guilty of serious misconduct, negligence or even criminal acts.

Since May 2008, when I took over the leadership of FAIR—a registered charity devoted to the protection of whistleblowers— I have been approached by more than 150 truth-tellers seeking help. They are from all parts of the country, in government and in the private sector, in senior positions or front-line workers. And the types of wrongdoing they describe vary greatly too. But one aspect of their stories is uncannily similar—the types of reprisal taken against them. It's as if there were a procedure, a standard game plan that the aggressors follow.

What I've learned from these conversations is that it's easy— childishly easy—for wrongdoers to cover their tracks and to silence witnesses, especially when the offenders hold positions of power and trust. Here's how it's done.

The most dangerous wrongdoers are not low-level employees who may pocket the petty cash, but middle and senior managers who engage in brazen, often well-planned schemes to further their own interests: contract fraud, grants to companies they own, payments for work that is never done, even policy decisions benefiting companies that reward them discreetly—and that they plan to work for after leaving the public service.

The [Canadian] Federal government spends more than $500-million every day. Even in fairly small departments it seems possible to skim off thousands, sometimes millions, without attracting attention—and in large departments much more. If someone can do this year after year, perhaps for decades, it soon adds up. Pretty soon we are talking about serious money.

Not all misconduct is financially driven: some wrongdoers are simply incompetent, malevolent, or self-absorbed who break much of what they touch, weaken their departments and make their employees' lives a misery—but they remain untouchable, protected by bosses who value their unswerving loyalty, or by close friends or family members in high places.

Preemptive Strikes

Smart wrongdoers stay alert to possible threats, such as employees who seem too idealistic, too independent-minded or too competent. Such potential whistleblowers are often singled out for special treatment even before they realize that there's anything amiss. The wrongdoer may take pains to remain on good terms with these individuals (or at least to keep them guessing) while rubbishing them to others: senior management, human resources staff and auditors. By the time the whistleblower discovers the misconduct and tries to raise the alarm he or she has long since been discredited—labeled as untrustworthy, a problem employee with a grudge or even mentally unbalanced.

Wrongdoers within the management ranks also hold some trump cards: their unchallenged authority over employees; control over management processes; and the reluctance of their superiors to face embarrassment.

The Milgram and Stanford Prison experiments, conducted in the 1960s and 1970s, demonstrated dramatically that most people are easily persuaded to "follow orders," to the extent of administering brutal, potentially lethal punishments to others— even when the person issuing the orders has no real authority or control over them.

When the person issuing the orders has real authority—by virtue of controlling subordinates' livelihood and careers—there seem to be virtually no limits. It's easy for a manager to isolate a suspected whistleblower, to threaten and humiliate them, and to engage other employees in such reprisals. Even close friends and colleagues of the employee may become afraid to be seen

Deterring Reprisals

To deter repetitive violations, those responsible for whistle-blower reprisal must be held accountable. Otherwise, managers have nothing to lose by doing the dirty work of harassment. The worst that will happen is they won't get away with it, and they may well be rewarded for trying. The most effective option to prevent retaliation is personal liability for punitive damages by those found responsible for violations. Another option is to allow whistleblowers to counterclaim for disciplinary action, including termination. In selective scenarios such as obstruction of justice, some nations, including Hungary and the United States, impose potential criminal liability for whistleblower retaliation.

Tom Devine, Tarek F. Maassarani, and Jeffrey Wigand, The Corporate Whistleblower's Survival Guide: A Handbook for Committing the Truth. *San Francisco, CA: Berrett-Koehler Publishers, 2011, p. 267.*

with them. Such harassment can inflict life-changing psychological injuries—leading to chronic depression, panic attacks, PTSD [post traumatic stress disorder], and even driving some to suicide. But dishonest managers can readily inflict this type of vengeance without even leaving "fingerprints"—it's all deniable as being beyond their control.

Wrongdoers in positions of authority can also manipulate management processes to protect themselves and to discredit witnesses. Records of the truth-teller's 20-year unblemished career may suddenly disappear from their personnel file, to be replaced with reprimands and bogus complaints. Absurd work assignments and rigged performance appraisals can also be used to create 'proof' that the whistleblower is incompetent, lazy or disobedient.

False accusations and retaliatory investigations are another tried-and-tested tactic, sometimes accusing the whistleblower of the very wrongdoing that they have tried to expose. And grievances can be manipulated too. Under Canadian law a grievance is considered a 'comprehensive remedy' for employees who complain of reprisals, so they have no other recourse—even when the grievance process is managed by the people who are accused of wrongdoing.

Top Management

As the cover-up and reprisals continue, top management often becomes implicated and committed to supporting the wrongdoers. This can happen in several ways: because the wrongdoers have persuaded top management into believing their version of the story; because the wrongdoing involves top management or reflects badly on them; or because top management has reflexively tried to minimize or ignore the problems in the past and now cannot turn back. That's why even good organizations, managed by honest and decent leaders, may engage in the most determined and contemptible reprisals.

Once top management is enlisted, however unwittingly, the entire resources of the organization can be deployed against the whistleblower, with devastating consequences.

Senior people may publicly malign the whistleblower's motives, character and mental stability. If a truth-teller initiates legal action, Justice Department lawyers are always assigned to defend the department—and their conduct in such cases too often smacks of revenge. The expression "heads on stakes" describes well the effect of such legal tactics—they send a stark warning to others.

Foreign Affairs whistleblower Joanna Gualtieri's lawsuit against her bosses for harassment was dragged out for 12 years, forcing her to answer more than 10,500 questions, until the judge ruled that government lawyers had abused the legal process. Since being fired, Dr. Shiv Chopra and his colleagues have spent 6 years in hearings before the Labour Relations Board and still have no ruling on their case. The government has paid more than $600,000 in fees to the now-retired manager accused of ordering their dismissal—to advise the legal team that is defending her actions.

Time is not on the whistleblowers' side. Given sufficient delay the wrongdoers will always win: the public forgets, evidence is lost or destroyed, witnesses move away or die, and the whistleblower finally collapses or gives up, exhausted—out of money and hope.

Soft Landings

It's hard for the public to understand why people guilty of blatant misconduct so often receive soft landings. It's usually for the protection of others.

When a wrongdoer is unmasked, top management generally wants to keep this as quiet as possible. Wrongdoers may be moved to other departments, perhaps with promotions and glowing references, or they may be paid off in some way that ensures their silence. Punishing them may not even be considered an option: it is likely to create embarrassing publicity; it may confirm that top management erred before in supporting a scoundrel; and the wrongdoer may still be vigorously protected by loyal and influential friends.

Above all it's often dangerous to punish the wrongdoer because he or she knows where the bodies are buried: if cornered, who knows what revelations might follow. We might never have learned about Brian Mulroney indiscreetly pocketing wads of cash had the former PM [Prime Minister] not abandoned and bad-mouthed Karlheinz Schreiber, leaving the former Airbus promoter vulnerable to extradition and jail.

Solutions for Justice

When we understand how wrongdoers operate and the advantages that they have, it is clear that unmasking them—and protecting whistleblowers—is a challenge.

But it can be done. Sheila Fraser's investigation has shown that misconduct in the highest places can be exposed when there is leadership and the will to do it—even when the law is unhelpful. Ouimet's is the first case of misconduct to be exposed through the legislation that she was charged with administering—after three years of zero results when Ouimet was calling the shots.

With a competent and proactive commissioner and a new properly-written law, Ouimet's agency can still become what it was supposed to be: a powerful deterrent against misconduct and corruption in government and a beacon of hope for honest public servants.

To this end, FAIR has launched a campaign entitled "No More Ouimets" that has the support of more than 30 government ethics organizations. We call upon the government to claw back Ouimet's $500,000 settlement package, to sanction her for failing to perform her job, and, above all, to rebuild the anticorruption agency that she was supposed to be creating.

Will this happen? It's entirely up to us. No important reform like this has ever come about without intense and unrelenting public pressure from citizens who believe that they can make a difference. Let's make our Canadian values of decency and honesty become a reality in Ottawa.

> *"By encouraging people to come forward with evidence of serious problems, the company can correct small problems before they become big problems."*

Organizations Do Not Help Themselves by Attacking Whistleblowers

Suzanne Lucas

Suzanne Lucas has worked as a human resources officer and is a columnist for BNET. In the following viewpoint, she argues that companies should encourage and protect whistleblowers. She says that doing so helps protect the company from lawsuits, catches problems before they become larger, and is also simply the ethical thing to do. She says, however, that companies may retaliate against whistleblowers for a number of reasons, including denial, fear, and a desire for profits. In the long run, however, she says, companies are better off when they listen to whistleblowers and act on their concerns.

As you read, consider the following questions:

1. What does Lucas say are the rational reasons for thinking that what a whistleblower says is not true?

2. According to Lucas, why are profits not a good reason to retaliate against whistleblowers?

3. What does Lucas argue that every company should have in order to manage whistleblowers?

You spot your company doing something illegal. You document the problem and take it to your manager and Human Resources department and they should support you, protect you and make sure the problem is fixed. There is a patchwork of laws surrounding this issue and they vary from state to state. But, of course, fixing the problem and protecting the whistleblower falls under the category of "right thing to do," no matter what state you live in.

The job of the Human Resources Department is to help the business be successful. By encouraging people to come forward with evidence of serious problems, the company can correct small problems before they become big problems that can result in serious legal and financial consequences for the company.

Apparently, someone forgot to tell certain Pharmaceutical Companies this. My *BNET* Colleague Jim Edwards writes:

> In a string of recent whistleblower cases a common theme has been the worried or disgruntled executive reporting wrongdoing to management, giving them the chance to fix the problem. Instead, management chose to harass or fire the staffer, thus virtually guaranteeing that a lawsuit would be filed.

I want to bang my head and say, "Why? What are you thinking? This exposes your company to lawsuits and fines and since you're pharma, illegal activities can actually kill people. WHHHHYYYY?" But, I'm a rational person and know why. It's not all about greed, either. (Although that undoubtedly plays a part.) Here are some of the non-obvious reasons why we punish instead of protecting.

Denial. It's a powerful thing. And there are rational reasons for simply denying that what the person is telling you is not true.

In the first place, you have no idea how often employees come forward complaining about "illegal" behavior that they see. My e-mail inbox is full of people wanting to know if it is "legal" for their boss to say, "nice dress," ask where they are going on vacation, require overtime, give a bad (but true) reference or any number of things that are absolutely legal.

It can make you jaded after a while. When everyone is knocking on your door claiming illegal activity is going on, and it's not, the temptation is to assume that everyone complaining is wrong.

Fear. No one wants to be the bearer of bad news. Do you want to waltz into the CEO's [chief executive officer's] office and tell him your sales reps have been selling pharmaceutical products off-label? Or that your expensive legal department approved language that violates several laws? No? Well, neither does your boss. It's easier to claim the whistleblower is the irrational one and causing disharmony amongst the ranks. You rarely need high level approval to fire a low level employee, but you sure as heck are going to have to tell the big boss in order to fix a systemic problem.

Profits. So, your drug is being marketed illegally. Sales reps are pushing an off-label use. But, it's selling well. If you stop this push, it will hurt sales, which will hurt the business, which may hurt your bonus, or worse, your job. So, if we can just keep this darn whistleblower quiet, or discredit him, life will be just fine.

Sure, no problem. Except, every day you continue to participate in illegal activities increases the chances you'll get busted. Especially if you harass the whistleblower. Most likely, this person will not only report your bad behavior to the relevant government agency, he'll initiate a lawsuit as well. The end result can be a lot more money lost then gained.

Misguided belief that it's not a big deal. So what if we're violating a law? People break the speed limit every day. What's the big deal? So, when someone comes forward, everyone says, "yeah, so what?" And then when that person complains again, people start to see the person as the problem, rather than the problem itself.

Forgetting about the big picture. Many people are so focused on their short term or departmental goals that they forget there is an entire company out there that will (hopefully) still be operating in 10 years. Focusing only on what brings in money *right now* causes you to neglect the fact that violation of laws may bring profits in the short run but will cause bigger problems in the long run. Sometimes you have to take the pain right now in order to preserve profits in the future.

Of course, these are just a few of the reasons Whistleblowers aren't taken seriously and are even punished. It should not be that way. Every company should have an established process for reporting and investigating problems. And, every employee should know how to report and have the reassurance that they will be listened to and not punished.

Communication lines should be kept open. If someone reports an activity that is within guidelines and laws, there should be follow up with that person to explain why. If a report is made that proves to be problematic, again, you should follow up and report back on how things are changing. Never ignore. That just makes people frustrated and angry.

And if you spot something going on that shouldn't be? You report it. Don't let yourself be caught up in the above justifications. It's always important to do the right thing.

*"On Wall Street, 'everyone
knows you play ball or live with
the consequences.'"*

For One Whistle-Blower, No Good Deed Goes Unpunished

Jesse Eisinger

Jesse Eisinger is a senior reporter on finance at ProPublica *and a columnist for the* New York Times. *In the following viewpoint, he says that Wall Street is hostile to whistleblowers. He points to the case of David Maris, an analyst who found evidence that a Canadian drug company was committing fraud and advised investors to sell the stock. For his honest assessment, which Eisinger says proved to be correct, Maris was sued, lost his job, and had his reputation among Wall Street firms damaged. Eisinger concludes that corporate culture in Wall Street is corrupt and broken.*

As you read, consider the following questions:

1. Why specifically did Maris put out a sell report on Biovail, according to Eisinger?
2. Why does Eisinger say that analysts rarely put sell ratings on stocks?
3. What does Eisinger say that Maris is doing now?

It has been noted repeatedly that almost no top bankers have faced serious consequences for their actions in the financial crisis. But there is a Wall Street corollary that might be even more pernicious: Good guys are punished.

Whistle-blowers, truth-tellers and fraud-spotters pay a miserable price on Wall Street. They are vilified. They are fired. Sometimes they are even sued. Instead of being sought after, they become persona non grata.

Recently, I caught up with David Maris, a one-time star pharmaceutical analyst for Bank of America who became embroiled in one of the most notorious bull/bear battles of the last decade. His story encapsulates just how broken Wall Street culture is.

In 2003, Mr. Maris put out a sell report on Biovail, a Canadian drug company. He fixed on the company's bizarre explanation of why it had missed its earnings estimates: A truck carrying a supposedly huge amount of medicine crashed at the very end of the quarter. Mr. Maris detailed why this was wildly implausible.

Desperate to deflect the attention, Biovail took the offensive. It sued Mr. Maris and Bank of America in early 2006. It also sued SAC Capital Advisors, the hedge fund, and Gradient Analytics, an independent research firm, claiming a giant conspiracy to drive down its stock price with false reports.

For a time, Bank of America stood by Mr. Maris. But it eventually caved and fired him—two weeks before the end of 2006, enabling it to not pay his bonus. Mr. Maris is now in arbitration, seeking $21 million in back pay.

"For the first few days, there were high-fives and a lot of media attention," Mr. Maris said. "People said this is what research should be. But then reality strikes the bank." Lawsuits and media coverage are unpleasant and unwanted.

Bank of America said: "Mr. Maris's departure was not connected to Biovail issues or to his research regarding that company. Bank of America values the independence of its research and has a longstanding practice of protecting that independence."

It turns out there was a fraud and a stock-manipulation scheme all along. But regulators said that it had been perpetrated by Biovail, not the analysts and hedge funds.

In March, Biovail settled with the Securities and Exchange Commission, which had accused the company and four current and former officers, including its former chief executive, Eugene Melnyk, of accounting fraud. Mr. Melnyk, who at one time was reported to be a billionaire, left in 2007.

Only this year, he settled with the SEC and the Canadian securities regulators, paying paltry fines. Biovail didn't admit or deny wrongdoing. (Biovail settled with the regulators over other, unrelated charges in 2008. The company merged last year with Valeant Pharmaceuticals International, losing the Biovail name.)

In recent years, Biovail retreated from virtually every allegation it made in its lawsuit. It dropped its claims against Mr. Maris and Bank of America in 2007. As part of a settlement, Mr. Maris agreed not to countersue.

The company also paid $10 million to SAC and forked over $138 million to settle a shareholder lawsuit.

So, here's the final Biovail vs. Maris scorecard: Mr. Maris was right on the facts. He was right on the stock. He was right with the law.

For his success, he was sued, fired and stripped of compensation. He also lost access to the world of bulge-bracket Wall Street, was shunned by some institutional investors, and because of the settlement that he said he felt he had no choice but to enter, he couldn't sue Biovail to seek vindication.

It's well known that analysts rarely put sell ratings on the stocks they cover. Typically, the explanation for this is that banks don't want to jeopardize their investment banking business.

The reality is much more complicated. Skeptics and whistleblowers risk huge career costs that go beyond conflicts of interest. Investors think they want unvarnished advice, but many don't truly appreciate it. Most banks don't want employees to

When I grow up, I'll apply these skills to my job on Wall Street.

play detective. Regulators abandon whistle-blowers, acting tardily and ineffectually.

After he was fired, Mr. Maris found that other big banks didn't want to hire him for research jobs. Even some institutional investors and hedge funds, which one might imagine would appreciate a skeptical voice, wanted no part of him. Many investors think an analyst who is picking fights with companies is a glory hound, and the last thing they want is publicity. No matter how frivolous, a lawsuit tars both sides. This is the "Tonya and Nancy" problem, after Tonya Harding and Nancy Kerrigan. One was linked to the perpetrators, and one was the victim. But now they are forever linked, and the difference between the two almost becomes blurred.

I don't want to create the impression that Mr. Maris is suffering. He isn't. He works at CLSA, a relatively unknown but important research shop, owned by a French bank that encourages its analysts to pursue independent lines of inquiry. Another analyst who has long been a truth-teller on banks, Mike Mayo, has also landed there.

But because Mr. Maris is willing to be publicly negative on stocks, he continues to face obstacles. He is prevented from asking questions on conference calls. Companies don't allow him to bring clients on visits. Some clients seem concerned about the lawsuits in his past.

"If you asked me what's my advice for a young analyst who wants to be in business for a long time, I wouldn't tell them to follow the path I went," he says. On Wall Street, "everyone knows you play ball or live with the consequences."

"Contracting officers now know that speaking up against contracting abuses will not bring them praise but can cost them their jobs."

An Expert in Government Contracting Faces Reprisals for Whistleblowing

Bunnatine H. Greenhouse

Bunnatine H. Greenhouse is a former contracting officer for the US Army Corps of Engineers. In 2005 she testified before Congress about fraud by Halliburton, a government contractor. In the following viewpoint, Greenhouse says that following her testimony, she was demoted, isolated, and subject to other reprisals. She says she was prevented from working to help in the aftermath of Hurricane Katrina, despite the fact that qualified personnel were needed. She concludes that her fate sent a strong message to other contracting officers that whistleblowing will be punished.

As you read, consider the following questions:

1. What does Greenhouse say she did in February 2003 after her objections to the Halliburton contract were ignored?

Bunnatine H. Greenhouse, "Testimony of Bunnatine H. Greenhouse at the Senate Democratic Policy Committee Hearing," National Whistleblower Center, September 21, 2007.

2. Who does Greenhouse say was moved into her position following her demotion?

3. According to Greenhouse, what specific reprisals has she experienced since her demotion?

My name is Bunnatine Greenhouse. I thank the Committee for allowing me to appear here today. As you may be aware, I was the United States Army Corps of Engineers' Procurement Executive and Principal Assistant Responsible for Contracting (PARC). I am the first black female to have held a Senior Executive Service [SES] position within the Army Corps of Engineers. A career spanning over 23 years ended on August 27, 2005, when I was removed from the Senior Executive Service and from contracting. I was removed after I raised concerns over the award of a $7 billion sole source, no compete, cost plus contract to Halliburton subsidiary Kellogg Brown & Root ("KBR") known as the Restore Iraqi Oil (RIO) contract. The award of this contract and other contracts related to the RIO contract represent the worst contract abuse I witnessed during my professional career.

Concerns About Contracts

Before the contract was awarded, I voiced great concern over the legality of the selection of KBR, the total lack of competition and the excessive duration of the RIO contract. I explained to representatives from the Department of Defense, the Department of the Army and the Army Corps that granting a contract for two base years with the potential to extend the contract for an additional three years was simply unconscionable under the compelling emergency justification that was identified as the basis for awarding the contract to KBR. All of my objections were ignored and so in February 2003 I chose to pen next to my signature on a critical contracting document my concern over the duration of the contract that was going to be awarded to Halliburton/KBR.

In October of 2004 I received notice that I was to be demoted and removed from the SES. At that juncture the concerns I had over the award of the RIO contract and other contract abuses related to Halliburton/KBR were brought to the attention of members of Congress and the public. In response to the substance of my concerns, the Acting Secretary of the Army directed that my concerns were to be referred to the Department of Defense Inspector General [DOD IG] for review and action and that I was not to be demoted or removed from the SES until "a sufficient record is available to address the specific matters" I had raised. Yet, the DOD IG has failed to conduct any investigation of my concerns.

In June of 2005 I was asked to appear before this Committee [the Senate Democratic Policy Committee] and I agreed to do so. Just prior to my appearance, the Army Corps' Acting General Counsel let me know in no uncertain terms that it would not be in my best interest to do so. I ignored this threat to my professional career and swiftly thereafter I was removed from the SES and from contracting.

Reprisals and Demotion

Things have not fared well for me since then.

After having a full year to figure out where I should be placed upon my demotion, I was directed to report to the Army Corps' Civil Works Engineering and Construction Division, where I was supposed to function as a "program manager." As I was about to report to the Engineering and Construction Division, Katrina was poised to strike New Orleans. Indeed, the horrific breach of the New Orleans levies [in 2005] commenced less than 24 hours from the time I was directed to report to the Civil Works division.

The response to the Katrina disaster was one of the largest contracting civil works efforts the Army Corps has ever faced. But, the Corps had no leadership in contracting; an SES was moved into my position who was not a Contracting Careerist and had not served a day as a contracting officer—and had to seek a waiver for the experience and training requirements that were established by Congress.

On the contracting side, I had long been acknowledged as the most knowledgeable and critical thinking contracting professional within the Army Corps, yet there was no role for me to play in response to Katrina.

On the civil works side, I am a Defense Systems Management College certified program manager, with a master's degree in engineering management from George Washington University, and a War College master's degree in national resources strategy, a master's degree in Business Management and a graduate of the Defense Senior Acquisition Course, yet there was no role for me to play in the face of the Katrina disaster.

Instead, I was systematically excluded from the Katrina management meetings that were held in my office area, behind closed doors.

I was born and raised in Louisiana and am a member of the Louisiana Hall of Fame for Women in Government, and I can assure you that it pained me greatly that I was not permitted to assist with the Katrina disaster.

Ultimately, the only reason given for having failed to give me performance standards for nine months was that my supervisor was too busy responding to the Katrina emergency to give me something to do. I don't believe that for one minute.

Isolation and Disrespect

Since my demotion I have experienced isolation; I continue to receive inappropriately down-graded performance reviews; my top secret clearance has been withdrawn; individuals have attempted to take credit for my work; no training opportunities have been identified since I have no Engineering and Construction mission responsibilities; and I have been prevented from returning to my contracting career field.

Additionally, I had to fight off efforts to cripple the Defense Base Act ("DBA") insurance pilot program—a program where I single-handedly wrote the concept of operations, and all solicitation documentation; responded to all questions from industry; conducted an industry forum with more than fifty insurance brokers in attendance; and engineered the procurement process to its final stages. The Congressional Budget Office has recognized the benefit of my DBA insurance program, which saved the government $45 million in its first year alone, with even greater savings forecast for the years to come. The intensity of the battle I had to fight to maintain the DBA insurance program leads me to believe that the Army Corps was more . . . willing to sacrifice my program than allow me to garner credit for its success.

Finally, it is paramount for this Committee to recognize that my removal has caused a deep chill to descend over the government contracting community and the SES Corps. Contracting officers now know that speaking up against contracting abuses will not bring them praise but can cost them their jobs.

Periodical and Internet Sources Bibliography

The following articles have been selected to supplement the diverse views presented in this chapter.

Marcus Baram	"Let's Ensure Whistleblowers Good Deeds Go Unpunished," *Huffington Post*, November 21, 2011. www.huffingtonpost.com
Dylan Blaylock	"MRAP Whistleblower to Return to Work," *Government Accountability Project*, November 16, 2011. www.whistleblower.org.
CBS News	"New Food Safety Law Protects Whistleblowers," February 11, 2011. www.cbsnews.com.
Julie Davis	"The House Cooks Up Another Turkey of a Bill, Guts Whistleblower Protections," *Examiner.com*, November 2, 2011.
Monica Davis	"Whistleblowers: Threatened, Killed, Neutralized—Silkwood, Hoare, and 10 BP Whistleblowers," *Before It's News*, December 1, 2011. http://beforeitsnews.com.
Tom Devine and Tarek F. Maasarani	"When a Whistleblower Makes the Call," *The Conference Board Review*, Summer 2011. www.tcbreview.com.
Thomas Drake and Jesselyn Radack	"A Surprising War on Leaks Under Obama," *Philly.com*, August 1, 2011. http://articles.philly.com.
Alan Judd and Heather Vogell	"Whistle-blowing Teachers Targeted," *Atlanta Journal-Constitution*, January 23, 2011. www.ajc.com.
Union of Concerned Scientists	"Protecting Scientist Whistleblowers," December 15, 2010. www.ucsusa.org.

For Further Discussion

Chapter 1

1. Kesselheim, et al., Kleinhempel, and Bisson all discuss possible moral and immoral motives for whistleblowers to report wrongdoing. Do you think it should matter what a whistleblower's motivations are in evaluating their charges? Explain your answer.

2. Awner and Dickins argue that reward programs do not motivate whistleblowers. Are there any other reasons to reward whistleblowers even if they are not motivated by money? Or should reward programs be discontinued if they do not motivate whistleblowers to come forward? Explain your answer.

Chapter 2

1. Are there any instances in which Schoenfeld would argue that government secrets *should* be revealed? Are there any instances in which Radack feels they *should not* be revealed? Is there any common ground at all between the two?

2. Having first read the viewpoints in this chapter, if you were Thomas Drake, would you have blown the whistle as he did?

Chapter 3

1. How is WikiLeaks different from earlier whistleblowers? Do these differences make it more effective or more dangerous?

2. Madar argues that knowledge is important for democracy and that Bradley Manning is a hero. Reagan, on the other hand, says that the public does not have the right to know everything and that Manning and Julian Assange are traitors. Who makes the more convincing argument? Explain your answer.

Chapter 4

1. Based on the viewpoints in this chapter, what benefits do organizations seem to get by going after whistleblowers? Do you think Lucas is right when she says that organizations hurt themselves by attacking whistleblowers? Explain your answer.

2. Imagine a friend has found evidence of fraud at the company where she works and is thinking about blowing the whistle. What advice would you give her? Consider reprisals she might face and steps she might take to defend herself.

Organizations to Contact

The editors have compiled the following list of organizations concerned with the issues debated in this book. The descriptions are derived from materials provided by the organizations. All have publications or information available for interested readers. The list was compiled on the date of publication of the present volume; names, addresses, phone and fax numbers, and e-mail and Internet addresses may change. Be aware that many organizations take several weeks or longer to respond to inquiries, so allow as much time as possible.

Bradley Manning Support Network
contact page: www.bradleymanning.org/ourwork/
contact-us
website: www.bradleymanning.org

The Bradley Manning Support Network is an organization dedicated to helping Bradley Manning, an Army intelligence analyst who was accused of releasing classified information to WikiLeaks and others. The support network advocates to mitigate the harsh conditions of Manning's imprisonment and to push for his release and acquittal. The website includes information on Manning, news articles, and information about events.

Center for American Progress
1333 H Street, NW, 10th Floor
Washington, DC 20005
(202) 682-1611 • fax: (202) 682-1867
e-mail: progress@americanprogress.org
website: www.americanprogress.org

Founded in 2003, the Center for American Progress (CAP) is a progressive think tank that researches, formulates, and advocates for a bold, progressive public policy agenda. The CAP website posts numerous website links and publications, including

"The Cables' Credibility Question" and "WikiLeaks Should Push Clarity on U.S. Strategy."

Government Accountability Project (GAP)
1612 K Street, NW Suite #1100
Washington, DC 20006
(202) 457-0034
e-mail: info@whistleblower.org
website: www.whistleblower.org

The Government Accountability Project is a nonprofit organization whose mission is to promote corporate and government accountability by protecting whistleblowers, advancing occupational free speech, and empowering citizen activists. GAP advocates for legislation to protect whistleblowers nationally and internationally and directs legal clinics for law students. It also monitors corporations and financial organizations, environmental agencies, and other key organizations and agencies. Its website includes discussions of its oversight programs and multimedia advocacy and opinion videos, as well as a regularly updated blog.

National Whistleblowers Center (NWC)
3238 P Street, NW
Washington, D.C. 20007
(202) 342-1903 • fax: (202) 342-1904
e-mail: contact@whistleblowers.org
website: www.whistleblowers.org

The NWC, and attorneys associated with it, support whistleblowers in the courts and before Congress. It advocates on behalf of whistleblowers and lobbies for laws protecting them. Its website includes policy discussions, press releases, and news reports.

Office of the Whistleblower Protection Program (OWPP)
Occupational Safety and Health Administration
200 Constitution Avenue, NW

Washington, DC 20210
(800) 321-OSHA (6742) • TTY: (877) 889-5627
website: www.whistleblowers.gov

OWPP, a program of the Occupational Safety and Health Administration (OSHA), is the program that administers the protection provisions of US whistleblower statutes. The OWPP website includes links to all whistleblower protection statutes, links to regulations, and instructions for filing complaints. It also includes OSHA publications on whistleblowing and links to press releases.

Open Government Initiative
1450 Pennsylvania Avenue, NW
Washington, DC 20230
(202) 208-1631
website: www.whitehouse.gov/open

The Open Government Initiative is a program by the Barack Obama administration to make government actions more transparent to the public. The website includes presidential statements on open government, blog news updates, progress reports, and more.

RAND Corporation
1776 Main Street, PO Box 2138
Santa Monica, CA 90407-2138
(310) 393-0411 • fax: (310) 393-4818
website: www.rand.org

The RAND Corporation is a nonprofit institution that helps improve policy and decision-making through research and analysis. The organization studies business and corporate ethics, among many other research topics. Its website includes content on whistleblowing, including "For Whom the Whistle Blows" and "How Whistleblower Rule Enables Corporate Compliance."

United States Department of Labor, Office of Administrative Law Judges, Whistleblower Collection

800 K Street, NW
Washington, DC 20001
(202) 693-7300
website: www.oalj.dol.gov

The US Department of Labor is the cabinet-level department responsible for employment and labor issues. The Office of Administrative Law Judges presides over formal hearings concerning many labor-related matters; its mission is to render fair and equitable decisions on these issues. The Whistleblower Collection includes significant decisions relating to whistleblowing, legislation relating to whistleblowing, links to laws and regulations, and research materials relating to whistleblowing.

Whistleblower Center

(800) 372-8313
website: www.whistleblowercenter.com

The Whistleblower Center is a network of legal resource sites, which provides visitors with news and information regarding whistleblower and false claims law. Its main goal is to help clients find experienced and trusted lawyers. The site includes information about whistleblowers, news updates, links to laws and regulation, and more.

WikiLeaks

Box 4080, Australia Post Office
University of Melbourne Branch
Victoria 3052 Australia
website: http://wikileaks.org

WikiLeaks is a not-for-profit media organization whose goal is to bring important news and information to the public. It provides an innovative, secure, and anonymous way for sources to leak information to its journalists, and one of its most important activities is to publish leaked original source material. Its website includes leaked materials as well as news reports and analysis.

Bibliography of Books

C. Fred Alford   *Whistleblowers: Broken Lives and Organizational Power*. Ithaca, NY: Cornell University Press, 2001.

Marek Arszulowicz and Wojciech Gasparski   *Whistleblowing: In Defense of Proper Action*. New Brunswick, NJ: Transaction Publishers, 2011.

Kathryn Bokovac and Cari Lynn   *The Whistleblower: Sex Trafficking, Military Contractors, and One Woman's Fight for Justice*. New York: Palgrave Macmillan, 2011.

Yoel Cohen   *The Whistleblower of Dimona: Israel, Vanunu, and the Bomb*. Teaneck, NJ: Holmes & Meier, 2003.

Cynthia Cooper   *Extraordinary Circumstances: The Journey of a Corporate Whistleblower*. Hoboken, NJ: John Wiley & Sons, 2008.

Tom Devine and Tarek F. Maassarani   *The Corporate Whistleblower's Survival Guide: A Handbook for Committing the Truth*. San Francisco, CA: Berrett-Koehler Publishers, 2011.

Daniel Domscheit-Berg	*Inside Wikileaks: My Time With Julian Assange at the World's Most Dangerous Website.* New York: Crown, 2011.
Daniel Ellsberg	*Secrets: A Memoir of Vietnam and the Pentagon Papers.* New York: Penguin, 2002.
Myron P. Glazer	*Whistleblowers.* New York: Basic Books, 1991.
Stephen M. Kohn	*Concepts and Procedures in Whistleblower Law.* Westport, CT: Praeger, 2000.
Stephen M. Kohn	*Whistleblower Law: A Guide to Legal Protections for Corporate Employees.* Westport, CT: Praeger, 2004.
Lian David Leigh and Luke Harding	*WikiLeaks: Inside Julian Assange's War on Secrecy.* New York: PublicAffairs, 2011.
Frederick D. Lipman	*Whistleblowers: Incentives, Disincentives, and Protection Strategies.* Hoboken, NJ: John Wiley & Sons, 2011.
Joel D. Hesch	*Reward: Collecting Millions for Reporting Tax Evasion, Your Complete Guide to the IRS Whistleblower Reward Program.* Lynchburg, VA: Liberty University Press, 2009.

Roberta Ann Johnson — *Whistleblowing: When It Works and Why.* Boulder: Lynne Rienner, 2003.

David Lewis, ed. — *Whistleblowing at Work*, New Brunswick, NJ: Athlone Press, 2001.

Marcia P. Miceli Janet Pollex Near, and Terry M. Dworkin. — *Whistle-Blowing in Organizations.* New York: Routledge Taylor & Francis Group, 2008.

Evgeny Morozov — *The Net Delusion: The Dark Side of Internet Freedom.* New York: PublicAffairs, 2011.

New York Times Staff — *Open Secrets: WikiLeaks, War, and American Diplomacy.* New York: Grove, 2011.

Peter Rost — *The Whistleblower: Confessions of a Healthcare Hitman.* Berkeley, CA: Soft Skull Press, 2006.

Micah L. Sifry — *WikiLeaks and the Age of Transparency.* New York: PublicAffairs, 2011.

Derigan Almong Silver — *National Security in the Courts: The Need for Secrecy vs. the Requirement of Transparency.* El Paso, TX: LFB Scholarly Publishing, 2010.

Wim
Vandekerckhove

Whistleblowing and Organizational Social Responsibility: A Global Assessment. Burlington, VT: Ashgate, 2006.

Robin Page West

Advising the Qui Tam Whistleblower. Chicago: ABA, 2001.

Daniel Wirls

Irrational Security: The Politics of Defense from Reagan to Obama. Baltimore, MD: John Hopkins University Press, 2010.

Index

A

Accounting fraud, 174

Adamu, Amos, 47, 48

Afghan War logs, 144

Afghanistan
kidnapping in, 84
US policies in, 134, 135
war in, 129–132, 145

Aftergood, Steven, 105–106, 109–110

Agribusiness intimidation tactics, 121, 122

Aid, Matthew, 110

Alias usage by whistleblowers, 100

Almajid, Phaedra, 47, 48

Alon, Gideon, 74

Altruism of whistleblowers, 28, 30, 42–43

American Journalism Review (magazine), 15

Ames, Aldrich, 103

Anaconda Wire & Cable Company, 55

Animal Policy Examiner (journal), 115

Anouma, Jacques, 47, 48

Antifraud laws, 52

Arab Spring revolutions, 126–127, 147

Arnold, Benedict, 153

Asian Football Confederation, 48

Assange, Julian
betrayal by, 153–154
high technology use by, 139–141
prosecution of, 154–155
sex assault charges against, 138
transparency and, 150
as WikiLeaks founder, 106, 129, 140

Associated Press, 121–122

Atomic Energy Commission, 158

Atta, Mohammad, 146

Awner, Jonathan L., 62–71

B

Bachrach, Judy, 126–127

Bahrain, 146

Balkin, Jack, 106

Baltimore Sun (newspaper), 103, 109–110

Bank of America, 173–174

Baquet, Dean, 86

Bartley, Hobart, 122

Ben Ali, Zine el Abidine, 126–127, 146

Berman, Howard, 56

Bernstein, Carl, 14

Betrayal vs. benefit of whistleblowers, 43–45, 153–154

Bin Hammam, Mohamed, 49

bin Laden, Osama, 106–107

Biovail report, 173–174

Birkenfeld, Bradley, 58, 60–61

Bisson, Mark, 46–49

Black, Hugo, 150

Blatter, Sepp, 48, 49

Bounties for whistleblowers, 67–69

Breuer, Lanny A., 98, 99, 104

Brian, Danielle, 107

Bruyea, Sean, 161–162

Buchanan, Patrick, 16

Bucy, Pamela, 51

Bush, George W. (administration)
actions against whistleblowers, 77
Iran attack by, 133

NSA security leaks and, 88–91, 104–105, 107–108
wiretapping by, 111, 113

C

Cambodian genocide, 16
Canadian Broadcast Corporation (CBC), 161
Canadian House Public Accounts Committee, 161
Canadian Labour Relations Board, 166
Caribbean Football Union (CFU), 49
Carnegie-Illinois Steel Corporation, 55
Centre for International Governance Innovation (CIGI), 137–142
Cheney, Dick, 133
Chicago Tribune (newspaper), 86
Chopra, Shiv, 161, 166
CIA (Central Intelligence Agency), 84, 103, 145, 147, 155
Civil War (US), 54, 55, 64
Clark, Thomas, 95
Classified information leaks
about NSA, 107–109
damage from, 109–110
obstruction of justice with, 99–101
over-classification of, 147–148
political reprisal over, 104–106
prosecution over, 102–113, 103–104
transmitting, 98–99
transparency vs. security, 106–107
unclassified vs., 110–113
See also National security leaks; WikiLeaks
Clinton, Bill, 79, 93–94

Clinton, Hillary, 127, 154
Colson, Chuck, 16
Comint Act, 77
Commodity fraud, 58–61
Compassion Over Killing, 115
Confederation of African Football, 47, 48
Congressional Budget Office (CBO), 181
Congressional Committee on Government Operations, 150
Contract fraud, 162
Court of Arbitration for Sport, 49
Crowley, Philip, 127
Cummings, Arthur M., 99

D

The Daily Show (TV program), 130
Damian, Sarah, 119–123
Danford, Hugh, 161
Data mining by wrongdoers, 108
Deep Throat (informant), 14–16
Defense Base Act (DBA), 180–181
Democratic National Committee, 14, 55
Dickins, Denise, 62–71
Divorce concerns with whistle-blowers, 34
Dodd-Frank Wall Street Reform and Consumer Protection Act (2010)
claims and bounties under, 67–69
eligibility under, 66
encouragement by, 63–64, 71
rewards under, 42, 44
Drake, Thomas
NSA leaks by, 90–91, 97–101
prosecution of, 95, 102–113

E

Eckard, Cheryl, 18
Edmonds, Sibel, 130

Edwards, Jim, 169
Egypt, 126, 146–147
Eisinger, Jesse, 172–176
Electronic Frontier Foundation, 108, 127
Eli Lilly and Company, 26t, 52–54
Ellsberg, Daniel
  background history of, 149–150
  as national hero, 140, 149–150
  Pentagon Papers leak by, 74–75, 139, 149
  prosecution of, 93
  WikiLeaks importance, 128–136
  See also Pentagon Papers case
Email accounts
  for global outreach, 142
  secure, 47, 99–100, 109
  of whistleblowers, 47, 99–100, 112
Espionage Act (1917)
  amending, 95
  against private citizens, 94
  prosecution under, 88, 93, 104
  as safeguard, 83
  violation of, 103, 106, 144, 154

F
False Claims Act (FCA)
  amendments to, 57–58, 64
  birth of, 54–56
  defined, 23
  monetary incentives under, 42
  overview, 52–54
  qui tam laws under, 51
  resurrection and, 56–57
  taxes, securities, commodities, 58–61
False Claims Reform Act, 56
FBI (Federal Bureau of Investigation)
  Deep Throat reveal, 15–16

  whistleblower prosecution by, 99–101
  whistleblower relations with, 32, 91
  WikiLeaks investigation by, 154
Federal Drug Administration, 69
Federal False Claims Act (FFCA)
  bounty program and, 64–65
  defined, 23, 64–65
  IRS data on, 69
  recoveries under, 68
  reports under, 70–71
  whistleblowers and, 67
Federation of American Scientists, 105
Feldstein, Mark, 14–15
Felt, Mark (Deep Throat), 15–16
FIFA (Fédération Internationale de Football Association), 47–49
First Amendment (US Constitution)
  House File (HF) 589 violation of, 115
  interpretation of, 77, 85, 89
  protection by, 86, 93
  protection of, 81
  violations of, 92, 115, 155
FISA Amendments Act (2008), 91
Florida Independent (newspaper), 120
Food Lion, 122
Foreign Corrupt Practices Act, 66
Foreign Intelligence Surveillance Act (FISA), 89–91, 107–108, 111
Fourth Amendment (US Constitution), 111
Fraser, Sheila, 167
Fraud cases/litigation
  accounting fraud, 174
  antifraud laws, 52
  awareness of, 71

contract fraud, 162
damage settlements, 58
in government, 56, 104–105
health care fraud, 21, 64, 68
overview, 21–22
against pharmaceutical companies, 23–26
policy implications, 35–39
qui tam and, 22–27, 51
recoveries from, 68
relators' accounts of, 27–35
reporting, 65, 68
with securities, 58–61, 174
study methods, 22
tax fraud, 58–61, 64
US Justice Department recoveries, 68, 70
whistleblower retaliation and, 54, 173
whistleblower rewards, 51, 55
Friedman, Brad, 128–136
From Colony to Superpower: A History of U.S. Foreign Policy (Herring), 147

G

Gates, Robert, 144, 147
Gee, Vernon, 121
General Accountability Project, 112, 122
General Accounting Office, 56
Gergen, David, 15
Gilmore, Scott, 139
GlaxoSmithKline, 18, 25*t*
Gorman, Siobhan, 103, 109, 112
Government contracting, 177–180
Government transparency, 104, 141
Gradient Analytics, 173
Graham, Laurie, 161
Grant, Colin, 18
Grassley, Chuck, 56

Graymail fears, 77
Greenhouse, Bunnatine H., 177–181
Gualtieri, Joanna, 165–166
The Guardian (newspaper), 126
Gurfein, Murray, 80

H

Haaretz (website), 74
Hague Machine, 55
Haig, Alexander, 15
Halliburton/KBR, 178–179
Handman, Laura, 109
Harding, Luke, 126
Harding, Tonya, 176
Hayatou, Issa, 47, 48
Haydon, Margaret, 161
Health Canada, 161
Health care fraud, 21, 64, 68
Heffernan, Margaret, 18–19
Heinbecker, Paul, 138, 139
Herring, George, 147
Hersh, Seymour, 79
Holder, Eric, Jr., 95
Howard, Jacob, 54–55
Hudson Institute, 104
Humane Farming Association, 122
Humane Society of the United States, 115, 123
Hunt, Andrew, 138, 139–140
Hussein, Saddam, 74
Hutton, David, 160–167

I

Illegal activity exposure, 87–96
See also Classified information leaks; Fraud cases/litigation; Wrongdoers
Informant Claims Program (ICP), 64, 65, 69–71
Intelligence Community Whistleblower Protection Act (1998), 91–92

Internal Revenue Service (IRS)
Informant Claims Program
(ICP), 64, 65, 69–71
whistleblowers and, 58–61
Iowa House File (HF) 589 bill,
115–117
Iran-Contra affair, 80, 89
Iraq
US policies in, 134
war document leaks from, 129,
131–132
war in, 133, 145–146
weapons development by, 74
Iraq War logs, 130, 144
Israel, 74–75
Israel Public Affairs Committee,
94

J

Jackson, Robert H., 77
Javers, Eamon, 18
Jennings, Peter, 85
Jobs/employment loss
over classified material, 110
identity issues with, 18
protection against, 52
rewards vs., 53
by whistleblowers, 28, 31, 32–
37, 39, 44, 108–109, 175
by wrongdoers, 43
Journal of Business Ethics (newspaper), 18
Journalists, unpatriotic, 85–86

K

Hurricane Katrina, 179–180
Keller, Bill
accountability issues, 86
NSA security breach, 107
prosecution of, 77–78
risks in publishing stories, 84
Kellogg Brown & Root (KBR), 178
Kennedy, John F., 85, 150

Kerr-McGee nuclear power plant,
158–159
Kerrigan, Nancy, 176
Kesselheim, Aaron S., 20–39
Klein, Mark, 108, 113
Kleinhempel, Matthias, 40–45
Kohn, Stephen Martin, 49–61

L

Lamo, Adrian, 131
Leigh, David, 126
Lichtblau, Eric, 107
Lincoln, Abraham, 54–55, 64
Lloyd-La Folette Act, 92
Los Alamos Science (journal), 158
Los Angeles Times (newspaper), 74
Louisiana Hall of Fame for Women
in Government, 180
Loyalty towards an organization,
41–42
Lucas, Suzanne, 168–171

M

Madar, Chase, 143–151
Madison, James, 150
Makris, Katerina Lorenzatos,
114–118
Malick, Mercy, 134
Management
behavior toward whistleblowers, 27, 41, 43–44
violations by wrongdoers, 92,
163–166
Manning, Bradley
betrayal by, 153–154
bin Laden, Osama, leaks by,
106–107
Espionage Act (1917) and, 144
as hero, 143–151
knowledge and democracy,
146–147
Middle East revolution leaks by,
126, 131

over-classification and, 147–148
prosecution of, 130–131,
154–155
supervision from, 144–146
transparency and, 148–151
Maris, David, 173–176
Mayer, Jane, 102–113
Mazuz, Menachem, 74
McArdle, Mark, 138, 140–141
McCarran, Pat, 95
McCarran-Walter Act, 95
Medicaid/Medicare programs, 53,
69
Mello, Michelle M., 20–39
Melnyk, Eugene, 174
Meotti, Giulio, 74
Mercy for Animals, 115
Merit Systems Protection Board, 91
Milgram and Stanford Prison ex-
periments, 163
Miller, Bradley, 122
Miniter, Brendan, 16
Morality issues
with national security leaks, 86
over Pentagon Papers, 133
strength requirements, 18–19
whistleblower motivation,
40–45
Morison, Samuel, 93
Moynihan, Daniel Patrick, 147
Mubarak, Hosni, 126–127, 146
Mullen, Michael, 135
Mulroney, Brian, 166

N
Narks as whistleblowers, 41
National food supplies
exposés on, 122–123
Iowa House File (HF) 589 bill,
115–117
law enforcement concerns,
117–118

overview, 114–115
pharmaceutical poisoning of,
161
whistleblower protection of,
119–123
National Security Agency (NSA)
declassification of documents
by, 147
disclosures to, 95–96
Drake, Thomas, indictment by,
98–99, 103
Office of Security and
Counterintelligence, 101
role of, 90
security breaches by, 107
spying on public by, 88
targets by, 111
National security leaks
danger of, 79–80
government discretion over,
83
illegal activity with, 87–96
morality issues with, 86
New York Times reports of,
88–93, 107, 110–111
overview, 74–75
the press and, 77–79
public opinion on, 82
punishing whistleblowers,
76–86
transparency concerns over,
80–83, 106–107
by unpatriotic journalists,
85–86
WikiLeaks and, 135–136
See also Classified information
leaks
Near v. Minnesota (1931), 85
Necessary Secrets (Schoenfeld), 88,
104
New Deal, 55

New York Times (newspaper)
  accountability concerns with,
    86
  Bush, George, actions against,
    77–78
  Felt, Mark, obituary, 15
  Kerr-McGhee's safety violations,
    158
  national security leaks, reports,
    88–93, 107, 110–111
Nigeria, 47
Nixon, Richard, 14–16, 109
Norman, Jim, 120
Nuclear power
  plant violations, 158–159
  weapons secrecy, 74–75, 133

O

Obama, Barack (administration)
  Arab Spring revolutions and,
    147
  espionage trial under, 95
  Medal of Freedom given by, 144
  NSA security leak, 107
  transparency concerns of,
    104–107
  whistleblower relations, 90, 113,
    148, 153
Obstruction of justice concerns,
  98–101, 164
Office of Security and
  Counterintelligence (NSA), 101
Official Secrets Act, 93
Ouimet, Christiane, 161–162, 167
Overman, Lee, 94

P

Pakistan, 131–134, 145
Patterson, Anne, 133
Pearson, John P., 101
Pentagon Papers case
  declassified, 147
  Espionage Act and, 93

Middle East parallels to, 133
  nature of, 129
  transparency concerns and,
    80–81
  WikiLeaks and, 129–132,
    139–141
  See also Ellsberg, Daniel
People (magazine), 158
People for the Ethical Treatment of
  Animals (PETA), 115, 120
Personal toll of whistleblowers,
  32–34
Petraeus, David, 132
Pfizer, 21
Pharmaceutical whistleblowers
  investigations into, 31–32
  motivations, 28–31
  overview, 18, 21–22
  penalties from, 52–53
  personal toll, 32–34
  policy implications, 35–39
  qui tam actions, 21–22, 23–30
  relators' accounts, 27–35
  settlements for, 34–35
  study methods, 23
Philadelphia Enquirer (newspaper),
  16
Pittman, Key, 94
Policy implications for whistleblowers, 35–39
Post traumatic stress disorder
  (PTSD), 164
Prendergast, Tom, 55
The press and national security,
  77–79
Principal Assistant Responsible for
  Contracting (PARC), 178
Project on Government Oversight,
  107
Project on Government Secrecy,
  105

Q

al Qaeda, 111, 134, 135–136
Qatar 2022 World Cup, 47, 48
Qatar Football Association, 48
Qui tam actions
  choices involved with, 38
  defined, 51–52, 59
  under False Claims Act (FCA),
    51
  fraud cases/litigation and,
    22–27, 51
  pharmaceutical whistleblowers
    and, 21–22, 23–30
  US Justice Department and,
    23–24, 38–39, 57
  whistleblower advice over,
    36–37
  whistleblower rights to, 57
  See also False Claims Act
    (FCA)

R

Radack, Jesselyn, 87–96, 112
Reagan, Michael, 152–155
Reagan, Ronald (administration),
  56, 57
Rehnquist, William, 15
Relators' accounts, pharmaceutical
  whistleblowers, 27–35
Religion as whistleblower motiva-
  tion, 18–19
Restore Iraqi Oil (RIO) contract,
  178
Revenge by whistleblowers, 43,
  46–49
Reward programs for whistle-
  blowers, 61–71
Risen, James, 79, 107
Roark, Diane, 109
Rohde, David, 84
Roosevelt, Franklin D., 85
Russo, Anthony, 93

Rutherford, Robert, 86

S

SAC Capital Advisors, 173
Saleh, Ali Abdullah, 132, 134
Sarbanes-Oxley Act of 2002
  (SOX), 63, 65–66
Schoenfeld, Gabriel, 76–86, 88–96,
  104
Schreiber, Karlheinz, 166
Schwarz Pharma, 69
Securities and Exchange
  Commission (SEC), 63, 174
Securities fraud, 58–61, 174
Senior Executive Service (SES),
  178
September 11, 2011, 79, 88, 106,
  139
Settlements for whistleblowers,
  34–35
Sheth, Sushil A., 69
Silkwood, Karen, 158–159
Simmons Foods, 121
60 Minutes (TV program), 122
Smith, Jeffrey H., 155
Snitches as whistleblowers, 41–42
Soccer. *See* FIFA
Soft landings of wrongdoers, 166
Stevens, Geoffrey, 138, 141
Stewart, Potter, 81–83
Studdert, David M., 20–39
Sunday Times (British newspaper),
  47–48
Sweeney, Annette, 114–118

T

Taliban terrorists, 84
Tamm, Thomas, 89, 113
Tax fraud, 58–61, 64
Taxpayers Against Fraud, 68
Top management implications,
  165–166
Traitors, WikiLeaks as, 152–155

Transparency
    advantage of, 44–45
    as American tradition, 148–151
    culture of, 43
    in government, 104, 141
    national security vs., 80–83,
        106–107
    promoting, 120
    risks from, 134
    secrecy vs., 80–83, 88
Transport Canada, 161
Truman, Harry, 95
Tunisia, 126–127, 146
Tyrrell, Steven, 112
Tyson Foods, 121

U
UBS tax scheme, 60, 70
United Kingdom's Parliamentary
    Select Committee Inquiry into
    Football Governance, 49
University of Alabama, 51
University of Kentucky, 147
US Army Corps of Engineers, 178
US Constitution. *See* First
    Amendment; Fourth
    Amendment
US Court of Appeals for the
    Federal Circuit, 91
US Department of Agriculture
    (USDA), 117, 122
US Department of Defense, 96,
    147, 178–179
US Department of Defense
    Inspector General, 179
US Department of the Treasury, 70
US Justice Department
    case settlements under, 27
    classified information compro-
        mised, 97–101
    Espionage Act violations, 154
    fraud recoveries, 68, 70

pharmaceutical investigations,
    27, 31–32, 53
    prosecution by, 31, 77, 80, 105
    qui tam actions, 23–24, 38–39,
        57
    secret surveillance, 95
    whistleblower law overview, 59
US satellite photo leaks, 93–94
US Senate Judiciary Committee
    Report, 51
US State Department, 126
US Supreme Court, 85
USA Today (newspaper), 108

V
Valeant Pharmaceuticals
    International, 174
Vandeveld, Darrel, 150
Vanunu, Mordechai, 74–75

W
Wainstein, Kenneth, 155
Wall Street and whistleblowers,
    172–176
Wall Street Journal (newspaper),
    16, 48, 109
Wallace, Mike, 85
War on terror, 77
Warner, Jack, 49
Washington Post (newspaper), 14
Watergate scandal, 14–15, 80, 89
Weapons of mass destruction
    (WMD), 78
Weather Underground (radical
    group), 16
Welch, William M., II, 101, 104
Whistleblower Protection Act
    (1989), 91, 92
Whistleblowers
    alias usage by, 100
    altruism of, 28, 30, 42–43
    betrayal vs. benefit, 43–45,
        153–154

Deep Throat (informant), 14–16
email accounts of, 47, 99–100, 112
encouraging, 63–64
graymail fears by, 77
management behavior toward, 27, 41, 43–44
narks as, 41
national food supplies and, 119–123
protection for, 66, 91–92
report increases, 68
snitches as, 41–42
targeting, 120–122
See also Classified information leaks; Drake, Thomas; Fraud cases/litigation; National security leaks; Pharmaceutical whistleblowers; WikiLeaks
Whistleblowers, consequences
attacks by organizations, 160–171
big picture concerns, 171
denial, 170
divorce concerns, 34
fear, 170
in government contracting, 177–181
isolation and disrespect, 180–181
job loss, 28, 31, 32–37, 39, 44, 108–109, 175
overview, 158–159
personal toll, 32–34
profit concerns, 170–171
prosecution, 79–84, 113
from Wall Street, 172–176
wrongdoer attacks, 160–167
See also National food supplies
Whistleblowers, motivation
altruism, 42–43

money, 42–43
moral vs. immoral, 40–45
program comparisons, 64–67
religion, 18–19
revenge, 43, 46–49
reward programs, 61–71
wrongdoer revelations by, 50–61, 160–167, 168–171
Whistleblowers, rewards
bounties, 67–69
do help, 50–61
do not help, 62–71
encouragement, 63–64
False Claims Act and, 52–56
IRS's ICP program, 69–70
as motivation, 70–71
overview, 50–52
program comparisons, 64–67
settlements for, 27, 34–35, 58
WikiLeaks
as dangerous to democracy, 137–142
Manning, Bradley documents on, 106–107
national security leaks and, 135–136
openness concerns over, 138–139
overview, 126–127
Pakistan conflict, 131–134
Pentagon Papers and, 129–132, 138–141
problems with, 140
risks from, 141–142
as traitors, 152–155
as vital to democracy, 128–136
Yemen conflict, 131–134
See also Manning, Bradley
Wilson, Woodrow, 150
Witt, Linda, 158
Woodward, Bob, 14–15

World War II, 55
Wrongdoers
    data mining by, 108
    job loss of, 43
    management violations by, 92,
      163–166
    preemptive strikes by, 163–165
    retaliation by, 164
    revelation of, 50–61, 160–167,
      168–171
    soft landings of, 166
    top management implications,
      165–166
    unmasking, 166–167
Wrongdoers, illegal activity
    debunked arguments, 89–91
    overview, 88
    protecting whistleblowers,
      91–92
    punishing, 95–96
    retrospective summary, 93–95
    security and secrecy, 88–89
Wyatt, Dean, 123
Wyda, James, 112–113

Y

Yemen, 131–134, 146
Ynetnews (website), 74
York, Jilian C., 127
*Youngstown Sheet & Tube Co. v.
    Sawyer* (1952), 95

Z

al-Zawahiri, Ayman, 146
Zyprexa (drug), 26*t*, 53